Rhoality
Guide to Wellness

James Circe

Rhoality
Guide to Wellness

James Circe

Published by Collin Oaks Winery

collinoakswinery.com

Copyright © 2024 Gary R Edwards

Printed in the United States of America

Second Edition

Other books by James Circe:

A Canopy of Angels

Power of the Quantum Mind

Wine, Flowers and Daydreams

The Ember Rose

The Cyrano Club

Passion Spent

The Very man

A Walk with the Shadows

ISBN: 9798862966695

Collin Oaks

In all my years of researching the human mind, I have found no part of the spiritual nature of man that could not be described by the quantum functioning of the brain.

Pashan

Table of Contents

Tables

Authors Note

There's reality and there's Rhoality (rō-al-ity). You're familiar with only the first one even though you live in both. One is presented to you through your five senses. The other, through vague and mysterious feelings and experiences.

Now, welcome to the world of Rhoality, our quantum connection to reality. Think serenity, wellness, and help for the future if you are one of the many who feel the inner connection with the world around you. If so, you know the pull that can only be explained by an understanding of how our universe was designed to allow our brains to work behind the scenes to help us out. Rhoality is an existence of leaning on this unseen but available powerful gift and using it to ensure a life of wellness and fulfillment.

Science has now proven what we call reality is a fairy tale fabricated by our brain but built on a science that had to be dumbed down so that our brains, powerful as they are, could comprehend. The real science is the quantum world that lies hidden in imperceptibly small bits of energy.

When we finally figured all that out, we discovered that we as humans weren't left adrift in a great sea of unforgiving nature. We were given access to information coming into our senses beyond the five we use most, to smooth our paths and guide our futures. For those who feel the pull and believe in themselves and reach out to others, the power is there.

Wellness is focused on the holistic way of living in a state of good health. More than that, a process for a lifestyle of necessary growth, a neutral state of balance, and a trouble-free mind is based on our brain as a caretaker, doctor, and guardian. You can be disease and pain-free, the perfect condition for the many facets of wellness - emotional, spiritual, physical, social, intellectual, environmental, occupational, and financial.

Your wellness journey through life began long before you were born. Your ancestors started fine-tuning your DNA countless eons ago. In all, despite being thrown into a jungle of unspeakable privation and violence, they did pretty well for you. Your body has trillions of tiny factories that not only produce the means to climb to the top of the food chain but the ability to ponder the wonders of our creation itself and even to look forward to a life of happiness.

You were conceived with the best body and mind your predecessors could manage for you. Their blueprint for your existence guides your physical formation. Although beyond your control, they did provide you with the tools of existence in some form. After birth, your own input creates the final product and that responsibility increases daily for much of your life. At some point you reach the state of knowing right from wrong, then it's all on you. There are lots of influences after that, but how they affect you and shape you is your call. Eventually, your bad judgments should lead to good judgment, but reactions based on emotion have unpredictable consequences and lead us astray. Without an inner base platform to retreat to, we can never fully trust our own judgment and often flounder through life.

Rhoality is a platform that provides a refuge for the mind to retreat to on any occasion, good or bad, mild or transformational. Based on the use of its quantum nature, it keeps us in tune with whatever power in the universe got us going at the start. It's all designed in us. It simply takes knowledge and belief to make it work.

The knowledge is found within the world of scientific experimentation. An excellent summary of the quantum functioning of the body is found in Circe's *Power of the Quantum Mind*.

The belief is trickier to come by. It comes from a state of an open mind that may have been written on by experiences that leave us stifled and mystified by looming disasters and failures brought about by forces beyond our control. What we might smile and imagine as a guardian angel is actually a result of unperceived forces that were designed into our brains that work for us when we allow them to.

The power of Rhoality is there for everyone. It can be brought out in all of us. This book will describe in detail how to determine and utilize the tools we're born with, taking as our main goal the best and highest use of our time on earth, based on a quiet faith in the future. Actually, that's the best definition of Rhoality.

Some readers will use this book as a reference document, so critical passages are repeated in various sections.

Introduction

Introduction

If we wouldn't mind letting fate determine our life, we could sell everything we own and bet it all on pass/no pass at the craps table and would have a 50% chance of either living a better life or becoming homeless. Instead, most of us like things that will return well over even odds. Not only does it reasonably leave us better off in the long run but the lower risk involved allows us to relax during the day and sleep at night. This is certainly a more pleasurable way to spend our time and keeps us healthier.

We don't talk much about the odds of success, but it pervades our thinking each time we make a decision, no matter how small. Predicting the weather, taking a job, making an approach to someone, we try to stack the deck in our favor ahead of time to increase the odds. Ah, if only we had more information about how things are, we could predict better.

So, in our reality world, when we have a big decision looming, we need to search for information, then find a quiet place where we

Rhoality Guide to Wellness

can ease our mind to think clearly, play out some scenarios to determine the actions we can take to follow the most likely path to success, then apply our moral code so we don't falter through guilty feelings. And apply the other emotions, like, do I really want to pay the cost it brings or will I be able to face others I out-compete?

Or, we can let our quantum brain do all this for us. After all, it has access to plenty of data we aren't even aware of, a quantum computer to work it all out and best of all, it's on our side.

Everything in our brain that allows us to think is called the mind. It contains a neural network that can calculate, store, and retrieve memories and analyze stimuli to know how to move our muscles and control our body functions. Some of these we are aware of, most not. The body has ways to alert our consciousness of changes through sensations (internal pain, five senses) and present our reality to us in useful ways, as in the video in our eyes we think of as reality. It

Introduction

is reprogrammable through learning experiences and logical analysis.

The part of the brain that works on a lower (quantum) level is hardwired to serve us without the conditions inherent in how we feel about things. It is easily overridden by emotions for those decisions where physical survival of the fittest isn't best served by being the strongest.

As we explore the ways we can use this quantum feature, we find that our brain requires belief in what we're thinking before it takes the right action. Some of us need scientific proof before we can truly believe, so each section in this book includes the science of what we just described. For those who prefer to not trudge into science, skip these sections and refer back to them when the seemingly magical process of Rhoality starts looking truly unbelievable.

The process starts with a familiar psychological mindset – positive thinking. It's not only powerful in itself but sets the stage for further functions that are more directed to the

Rhoality Guide to Wellness

subconscious mind, which is 95% of brain activity.

Then, after negative thinking is corrected, a process called Entrex provides a serene body for the brain to work with. We then explore the healing power of the brain itself and introduce the quantum functioning of the brain that is the real magic in modern medical science. Understanding that these once-considered miracles are actually proven science leads to belief, which is the base ingredient for the brain to achieve what it does.

The final feature in the process is Rhoality envisioning. This method allows us to use quantum science to make amazingly accurate predictions to increase the probable success of future happenings, what are called end events, thus allowing us some say-so in how they turn out.

One

Think

and

Grow Healthy

Rhoality Guide to Wellness

Positive Thinking

It all starts with achieving a balanced brain, one that was designed to be able to create a reality in our mind. Our body, along with nature, our senses, memory, and reasoning power, all are there to provide consistency in how the things that happen to us work. Science has worked its way to the bottom of it all and found energy. It creates magnetism which allows clumps of energy to glow, making us think that things we call matter really are what they look like. That fools us into thinking our reality world isn't a fantasy.

In all, it works for us, as long as the rules are comprehensible and allow our fantasy bodies to provide us with maybe a hundred years of living. We do our best with what we are given and experience as many pleasurable events as we can. Being somewhat clever, we realize that misuse of our physical systems will eventually put an early end to that.

So, how to stay healthy for life. Rhoality allows us to follow a life process that moves us along a

Think and Grow Healthy

path that lets us end up at the maximum achievement point that the luck-of-the-draw inheritance from our ancestors will allow. It's not risk-free. In fact, it encourages risk up to the level that any higher amount would cloud our judgment, thus lowering the probability of success.

The simple act of thinking positive thoughts has a power all its own. A healthy, well-rested body and mind make for rational decisions. The power of positive thinking is motivation to get going and make things happen. It gives us the confidence to push against obstacles, molding other people's perception that they should help move barriers out of our way and overlook the bad that we do and that we will do good things for them.

Rhoality Guide to Wellness

It will:

- Make you feel better, more relaxed, more able and willing to move from your current situation.
- Clean your body of tensions that affect health.
- Clear your brain to think straight.
- Snap off the downward spiral of negative what-ifs.
- Put a pleasant look to your face that allows others to be more comfortable talking to you and stops them from building a wall or perceiving a threat, however small or trivial.
- Free up energy to your muscles to enable you to stand tall.
- Fill your brain with energy to have better decision- making and memory use.
- Encourage others to help you in your trials or at least not take action that hinders you.

When you add Entrex (next chapter) to the positive mind, your body stays healthy and balanced. Your mind is coherent and confidence is heightened, allowing you to meet these objectives:

Think and Grow Healthy

- Do your best.
- Look your best.
- Stay healthy.
- Feel esteemed and loved.
- Experience pleasure often.
- Feel good – avoid depression.
- Control brain miscues.
- Have no chronic worry, anger or guilt.
- Avoid mental and physical trauma.
- Stay off unnecessary medicine.
- Find purpose in life.
- Have a quiet faith in the future.
- Live well until you die.

Note here that these are all reality level and mostly based on one's personal feelings, both mental and physical. None require the input or aid of others even though they are generally defined by our perception of others' emotional reactions to us.

If there is a supreme intelligence that meddles in our affairs, it is relegated to sitting on our shoulder whispering encouraging words in our ear. Our quantum mind does the rest.

Rhoality Guide to Wellness

.

Thinking negative thoughts

When you entertain bad thoughts, you give them life in your mind. Your attitude affects people and events around you, both actively and passively, by commission and omission. Others react to your state of mind, causing them to become a part, perhaps a creator, of the bad end events that you had envisioned. Your health is affected, which changes your interests and actions, lessening the strength of your daily support system. Indeed, you invoke Murphy's second law: *The more you fear something, the more likely it is to happen.*

Negative people are a drain on themselves and you. When we dwell on a bad thing that can happen, we give it priority in our minds as a sort of shock, then look for a quick way to avoid it. We dig deep into our memories to flush out the what-ifs. Our emotions turn to worry, then fear, about the dreadful consequences. Many people try to manipulate us using chronic worry, anger, and guilt.

Think and Grow Healthy

The more frustrated we become in life, the quicker the negative response arises. If we are accused, we seek retribution. If offended, pay back. If wronged, revenge.

Negative thoughts are only useful as a motivator to make us realize how bad things could be if we don't do something.

Intuition and instinct

When we quickly react to a stimulus without conscious thinking, we don't call it a spiritual event. We label it as instinct or intuition.

Intuition begins as an unconscious awareness of the use of the brain's quantum feature to set events up in our favor and are only slightly leaked into our consciousness. We aren't given details because they are uncertain, just the knowledge that a path to our end event is available and being prepared for us.

Rhoality Guide to Wellness

Intuition is our ability to understand without conscious reasoning or even evidence. It manifests itself as a slight feeling that somehow, we have connected with the cosmos. Instinct is more hard-wired into our brain and relies on past, present, and future knowledge. Both are able to generate solutions without conscious data analysis when small bits of reality make their way into consciousness. Some people have to learn to recognize it while others have a more prominent awareness.

Instinct is even more detectable in animals. A bird can weave a nest without training from its parents and with no trial and error. It even knows which building material to select, just the right length and pliability, weather-resistant strands and works them until it is as well built as could be possible. All is DNA driven, stored in their brains by some unknown ancestors.

Instinct and intuition both come to us from our ability to make use of our parents' DNA. Our brains are full of it from that makeup.

Think and Grow Healthy

People who are highly intuitive are ones who have learned to listen for and recognize the information that Rhoality has dug out and made available to the conscious mind. They have a high degree of trust in its ability to provide desired results for a clearer understanding of how we use it in the future. Holistic health involves a person's physical, mental, emotional, intellectual, and spiritual leanings. Intellectual curiosity is often called a spiritual thing that opens the door to Rhoality-based intuition.

The intuition your parents gave you isn't all that different from the DNA that your caveman ancestors gave their children. Since the capacity for information storage in DNA is mind-boggling, this modern DNA has soaked up knowledge of not only past events but also the results of their DNA being altered to facilitate survival through mutations and the rewiring of the subconscious mind. The quantum nature of the brain allows for quick storage and conversely, retrieval of this information. People who have memories of a past life are tapping into this stored data, mistaking it for their own bygone life.

Rhoality Guide to Wellness

The thoughts and actions of our parents cascaded through their minds over many years. That information was absorbed by the energy and DNA in their brains, determining instinct. If they experienced an intimate or traumatic moment or situation, our ability to access those events is increased because we hold tiny bits of DNA from each of our vast number of ancestors. Unfortunately, if our parents were of a meek nature, they were likely full of fear, shame, and doubt. That reinforces not only those mind miscues but also nightmares, trauma, and depression.

Compassion

Compassion calms the mind and takes us out of our stressful tension. This form of relief fills our worry and fear buckets with someone else's problems. We can decide to ignore the bucket, but that leaves it simmering inside us. Replacing it with compassion reduces the boiler roiling.

Think and Grow Healthy

It may be that we give compassion, along with love and gratitude, because it lays an obligation on the receiver to consider having a reason to do us good, or at least to not do us bad. Then compassion would be a shot of relief for ourselves. An emotion, such as fear, that spurs us to act in our own self-interest, is a chance to demonstrate to the world that we have value and is a way to force a connection with someone else.

Intellectual Curiosity

With intellectual curiosity, we look for that tiny spark that comes with the intuitive feeling, which some say is the same. When we think of something that isn't known to us, we just want to understand it. The same desire opens our mind to stimuli beyond the brain's memory and input from the five senses. Anyone with intellectual curiosity can be highly intuitive if they allow their curiosity to override the innate fear of the unknown.

Rhoality Guide to Wellness

Curiosity forces us to question everything. How does that work? What's happening? Who made that? Where did it come from? What happens if it goes the other way? How do they fit together? What's behind the statement? Note that this curiosity and a closed mind are mutually incompatible. Can you close your mind about one thing yet be totally open for others?

There is a negative side to curiosity. You must apply foresight and sensitivity or else you will be driven to an unwanted conclusion just to see what happens. Curiosity pushes the risk factor higher because the lure of learning the result of actions is a significant reward for the increased risk. This is especially true in personal interactions.

Entrex

Entrex

Rhoality Guide to Wellness

In 2020, I delved into meditation to get a clearer look at the way I had taught myself to react to unexpected events. Misfortunes to people close to me impelled me to want to draw a clearer sense of my role in their lives. I found myself deep into my subconscious mind, where the automatic responses are stored. It wasn't a pretty picture. Work was needed there.

At about the same time, I realized that I had been having a fortunate series of healing touches, even though I was unaware at the time of their positive effect on the balance and coherence of my mind. Through their entraining healing power, I was able to create inner resonance so that I could begin work on replacing the toxic set of stimuli responses that were accumulated over a lifetime with ones that are calmer, more reasoned, and acceptable to other people.

Progress was cut short the next year when a tiny ringing in my ears created a continual storm in my mind. No longer able to get into the right

Entrex

mental state for meditation, I realized I needed to solve the daily increasing tinnitus before it overtook me. Its start date wasn't hard to pin down since it was the same week I received my second virus vaccine shot. I kept a journal on how it cycled through my mind, increasing in volume until eight months later I wrote that it was like someone standing next to me, shouting into my ear. Something had to give.

Finally, I began to see a pattern arise with the volume being louder at times of stress and diminishing as I began relaxation trials. Strangely enough, it corresponded more with the pressure I could put on my brain through the craniospinal fluid (CSF) than through my blood pressure, the usual gremlin. When I tried massing energy in my brain, dizziness resulted. When I went through lower-muscle relaxation, the dizziness abated and eventually, the ringing dimmed. After a further two months, I was able to control the ringing totally by quickly applying my long-used relaxation process I call Entrex.

Rhoality Guide to Wellness

Entrex: the process of relaxing the lower enteric area muscles to complete survival mode cleansing.

Survival Mode Cleansing

The key to maintaining balance in the body is to fully cleanse it of stress that is created when the body goes into its survival mode. In modern times, stress is a constant companion and total escape from the survival mode is rarely accomplished.

This requires a fully relaxed set of organs that are connected and controlled by the vagus nerve. This nerve runs from the brain to the colon. It connects to all the muscles that allow the brain to orchestrate a fight-or-flight decision. This includes control of the lower muscles in the area below the end of the intestines, called the pelvic floor, to dampen all waste and procreation management. These muscles can be consciously stressed and relaxed at will by the conscious mind, using a process

Entrex

called enteric relaxation (Entrex). It completes the survival mode cleansing and allows the brain to relax any organs that didn't get the message to recover.

Pressure by an enteric stress push, the opposite of a relaxation, arrives in the brain by a direct route. This process involves the CSF that circulates (mostly down) from the brain to the lower intestinal area and back. Pressure applied to the pelvic floor area affects the brain quickly. This path carries fluid to many organs including the pineal gland, where piezoelectric calcite crystals create a magnetic field due to the pressure exerted on it by the enteric push. Since the brain is full of CSF, constant pressure added to it can result in dizziness and a host of other brain-created and directed dysfunctions.

The brain reacts to this pressure as it would a survival message from the five senses by ordering a slowdown of vital organs. This impedes the blood supply that sustains them and slows toxin removal. Only when the vagus system is fully relaxed are these organs allowed to resume normal functioning. Meanwhile, the

Rhoality Guide to Wellness

toxins and lack of blood disrupt the normal cell actions and can lead to inflammation, which could result in organ disfunction and eventual failure.

Handling Brain Miscues

Staying in a partial survival mode confuses the brain and is the root cause of brain demons like insomnia, constipation, tension headaches, muscle cramps, ear ringing, dizziness, hiccups, some sneezes, and possibly all brain-induced malfunctions of the body. These may all be able to be prevented or halted as they get started by an Entrex. In fact, each of these is a signal from the unconscious mind to the conscious mind that an Entrex is needed.

How to Perform an Entrex

Relax, close your eyes, clear your mind, and open your ears, to shut out all external stimuli

Entrex

other than what your brain is sending to your ears. This allows you to focus your attention on your muscle relaxation. First, let go of the stomach muscles, then on down to your tailbone. You will feel the relaxation in your pelvic floor muscles and in your mind. Concentrate on the muscles. This is a conscious action, so it will require your full concentration while you slide into a fully relaxed stage. When you feel that the muscles are relaxed, move your focus to what your brain is sending to your ears. Stay there as long as possible. Twenty minutes is ideal but even a few seconds works wonders. Try to stay awake because the sleep state recovery by the mind replaces the pressure on the muscles. If that happens after a successful session, it should be possible to reestablish the Entrex in short order.

If you are using Entrex to ease a headache or muscle spasm, the results speak for themselves. If simply trying to ease tension, when you arrive at that state and return to the outer world, the feeling of release from anxiety manifests as

Rhoality Guide to Wellness

gratitude, love, self-actualization, and an overall joyful peace.

Three

Brain Healing

Rhoality Guide to Wellness

We will cover stress as a cause of disease, body needs including diet, coherence, balance, and brain rewiring, then the placebo effect, belief, brain chemicals, and touching others as a healer.

A Healthy Brain

The brain is powerful enough to heal and maintain the health of the body. Its quantum ability can access any and all event information stored in the ubiquitous energy field that surrounds us (and possibly of the entire universe) and calculate the most probable results of actions taken, considering its intimate knowledge of its own state. This is called predicting the future from the past and can get close to 100%. For more information on predicting, refer to Appendix A.

Anxiety is our normal companion, served by chronic stress, which is what prevents the brain from keeping the body healthy. The brain can only do its job properly when it is balanced and

Brain Healing

coherent. It is constantly barraged by stimuli arriving through the senses, warning signals from organs and nerves, and survival programming running in the background and constantly crying for attention that must be attended to. A healthy body, serene surroundings, and a return to positive thinking can maximize the brain's ability to tend to us.

To survive in an ever-changing and always danger-packed world, the brain can marshal its response quickly. This gives extra energy to the physical parts of the body that can repel or evade potential damage from external stimuli. The initial subconscious tension redirects the blood supply and dumps energy-producing adrenaline into the muscles. But the parts that are being shorted cannot do so for a long period of time without damage. The body, and especially the brain, must remove the survival-level chemicals and return to its calm, cool, and collected state. Otherwise, a brain that is still receiving danger stimuli from its internal organs will miscalculate the administration of chemicals that not only provide the process of fuel and air into energy but also direct toxin removal and normal maintenance functioning.

The body, through the mind, speaks to us emotionally as conscience and physically as pain. Our bodies are normally full of drugs that allow us to cope with whatever ails us but prevent brain balance. If you take a painkiller pill instead of fixing the cause of the pain, you train your brain to expect an outside fix instead of handling the problem itself.

The brain can recognize and handle viruses and bacteria. It has a tougher time with toxic chemicals, which attack and destroy cells. How a simple organism like a virus can change itself to be able to fool the body's immune system to force its way into cells is surely part of the original design that needed a mechanism to evolve life.

The brain can keep the body healthy and prevent all brain-induced maladies, including autoimmune diseases, with almost no external chemical supplement added. The only

Brain Healing

exceptions are trauma resulting in physical damage to the body parts and certain virus-type organisms that are able to fool the brain (but not a coherent one).

The brain is undoubtedly the best pharmaceutical supply in existence. Not only can it manufacture every medicinal chemical the body needs to stay healthy, but it does so with perfect selection and efficiency. When coherent, it constantly analyzes the vast amount of data from all parts of the body (trillions of cells).

The brain can heal the body, but first, you must heal the brain.

Stress as a Cause of Disease

Anxieties are fed by chronic worry, anger, and guilt. The meta-science of psychology describes mental states of reality that handle our stress responses for us by altering and directing brain energy.

Rhoality Guide to Wellness

Organ dysfunction is mostly due to false instruction from the brain, causing inflammation.

There is a level of stress below which we need to aim. Hunger brings immediate stress. Lust, safety, higher needs like esteem, all pull us out of a calm state. Our brains are attuned to these needs and guide us to their satisfaction, but at some point, we are in danger or wanting more than we can handle, which creates a probability of a high risk of anxiety.

The goal of life as described herein results in zero chronic stress, which has several forms. It can manifest itself as a motivator or a destroyer.

- Zero stress, daydreaming, joyous feeling from pleasure, Rho State (theta, alpha, relief). Think about what the moments of stillness have meant to your life.
- Useful stress, focus our awareness on the problem. Go into survival mode to gather

Brain Healing

energy and see a chance for the pleasure of doing fun things. Coming out of survival mode causes us to pay attention to non-local events. It also increases our knowledge, our memories, and our confidence in our ability to solve problems. We use this new feeling level to raise our quiet confidence level.

- Wasteful stress - adds anxiety since it is above our quiet confidence level. Risks damage to organs and even failure. Is sometimes not avoidable since most stimuli are non-local. Must be short-lived by returning to coherence for decision-making.

Inflammation caused by stress can cause heart disease, diabetes stroke, and liver failure. Others are dementia, cancer, fibromyalgia, autoimmune rheumatoid arthritis, multiple sclerosis, and thyroid disorders.

Destressors:
- Intuition
- Love
- Creativity
- Meditation

Rhoality Guide to Wellness

- Beauty
- Appreciation
- Gratitude
- Compassion
- Serenity.

In summary, stress is what prevents the brain from keeping the body healthy. The brain can only do its job properly when it is balanced and coherent. Stimuli arriving through the senses, warning signals from organs and nerves, and survival programming running in the background are constantly crying for attention and must be attended to. The health and serenity of returning to the Rho state can maximize the brain's power to fight disease.

Meeting Body Needs

Disease comes from too much or too little attention to the body system. Balance is the key as well as prevention. It promotes harmony and

Brain Healing

resonance in the body's biofield, which is the aura around the body.

If you're not set on giving your body what it needs: nutrition, movement, and serenity every day, then no wellness option will ever work fully. You may eventually turn to drugs or medicine of some sort to keep you functioning in a sort of pain-free existence while blocking your own brain from coming to your aid. So, the steps to pursue are diet, movement, positive reinforcement, Entrex, envisioning, rewiring the subconscious, and seeking others.

Diet

Food contains the best medicine, both preservative and active, since man first evolved. It provides the nutrients and active chemicals to keep the body healthy in an extreme environment. The brain cannot balance when part of the body is off balance. So, start there

Rhoality Guide to Wellness

and become accustomed to a proper diet before you venture further into Rhoality.

Nature took great pains to set it up. When you dutifully see to it that your body has the nutrition and other foodstuff that it needs, you set the stage for other good things like pleasures and avoiding conflict. When you live in a Rho state, you maximize the amount of time you have to spend attaining and less time overcoming.

It's hard for the brain to overcome the toxicity of our diet. With nutrition, it will develop a process to keep the brain balanced and coherent. There is no reason why you should not maintain health as long as your body is physically undamaged by injury or normal aging. There are no guarantees of a long life but the enjoyment of health during it all Is the best it gets and is priceless.

Brain Healing

Movement

Along with diet, keeping the body active, however you define your motions, which can be exercise, fitness, or simply never sitting still, is a basic necessity. Movement is just putting your body through whatever actions that keep it functioning at the level you live at. The goal is to not only prevent muscle atrophy but also a wide variety of other health benefits.

If you lack either diet or movement, stop reading and go get ready. Don't start reading again until you're physically on your way to being the best you can be.

Placebo Effect

A placebo is a harmless substance given to a patient in place of real medicine to make them believe they are being treated. The placebo effect was discovered when an army doctor ran

Rhoality Guide to Wellness

out of morphine but told the wounded soldier that the fake medicine he was getting was the real thing. It worked.

The patient's brain was convinced that it had gotten morphine, so it stopped the pain. This is particularly true for problems that the brain itself actually creates.

Patients must believe that they were given the good stuff. The key to the placebo working is the belief of the mind. In fact, belief is key to all mental level healing. Fortunately, there is now scientific proof of its efficacy. Often if the drug has an expected side effect, the patient is given a drug that mimics the expected effect. At times they may have to be conditioned into believing by altering the pill's looks or taste.

Studies have demonstrated that thinking of a treatment produces the same effect as the treatment. Once the mind actually believes that it has been given the medicine, it secretes the same chemicals as it would have when the medicine was actually administered. Along with this, experiments have shown that people can

Brain Healing

decrease their pain levels by thought alone by actually producing the chemicals that block pain in the body after it works for them once and they believe in the power of the brain. However, the brain will take no action to produce a cure if it doubts itself. The small percentage of those who see no improvement are almost assuredly the result of a confused or unbelieving mind.

In summary, to heal the body, the brain must be balanced. Belief is paramount. Homeostasis is the optimal condition of the body. It is the chemicals that the brain creates to fight the virus, not the chemicals we're injected with, that do the job.

Four

Rhoality

and the

Quantum Brain

Quantum Brain

The Quantum World

Get Real! Put yourself into the ultimate world of sanity and reason, and believe what your eyes are telling you. Tie your anchor to this solid rock we all use to measure ourselves and base decisions for our futures.

Actually, this paragon of scientific dogma began crumbling over a hundred years ago when we gained the ability to see down into the microcosm of quantum science. It revealed not only cracks in what we believe to be the truth, but a seemingly uncrossable chasm.

We, as logical human beings, have reasonably elevated reality to the honored position of absolute truth. But who says it isn't? Quantum science does.

In the past, science has often let its hubris overwhelm our good sense, thinking and proclaiming aloud that we understand how the universe works. But now with the blossoming of quantum physics, we finally admit that we will

Rhoality Guide to Wellness

never know it all. Our conscious minds are simply too . . . well, simple, to comprehend.

Maybe that's not such a big problem. If we can sort out enough of it, we can use it to improve our reality. That can be OK, and probably the best we can hope for. Can our brain's quantum abilities be accessed to do so? Yes, it's a process called Rhoality, and this book tells us how to make it work.

Objective

We will discuss the quantum facts involving two things being in one place at the same time (superposition), one thing being in two places at the same time (entanglement), quantum computers (that simulate the brains' computers), the quantum nature of particles and how they work in our brain, quantum collapse by an observer, all as a basis for this chapter (brain healing of the body). If you are already familiar with these concepts, you might

Quantum Brain

want to move on to the next chapter, on envisioning.

It is hard to have absolute belief in the Rhoality process without some level of knowledge in the seeming magical functioning of quantum workings. This is a good place to get familiar with them. Table 1 gives a short description of quantum features in the simplified form used here.

Rhoality Guide to Wellness

Table 1. Basic Quantum Features

Entanglement	Two particles that are quantum entangled detect any event that happens to either one the same as if it had happened to them both.
Superposition	The ability of particles to be in more than one place at a time in the quantum world.
Quantum collapse	Matter begins existence as a cloud of possibilities. Observing it causes it to collapse to one of the possible states. The term quantum collapse means selection of one of many possibilities.
Observer Collapse	In quantum physics, no result is turned into reality until it is observed by a consciousness.

Quantum Brain

Quantum Physics in a Nutshell.

So, if the real world we live in isn't the truth, where does it come from? Start with what was here before the cosmic Big Bang created our universe. Everything was a sea of vibrating energy, most likely tiny strings. They moved in frequencies so diverse that a video machine like our brain would not be able to discern, let alone make use of the information stored there. So, something squeezed a bit of it together, creating an explosion that sent some of it into a state that atoms could eventually form as magnetic dots that could be manipulated into things. Things like stars and tables and trees, even us. But no use going through all this if there's no one there to appreciate it all. So, brains were invented (or, by chance, even though science says it is so improbable as to be impossible).

By the time our brains came into existence, most other things were already here. A diverse set of atoms gave out energy (light, or more scientific, photons), that could be detected and

Rhoality Guide to Wellness

analyzed. We call these atoms matter, though they're almost completely space. Each atom has a nucleus surrounded by one or more electrons. If you blew up an atom in size to where the nucleus was the size of a basketball, the electron would be over two miles away. What we think of as hard surfaces are almost all space, held together and kept shaped by basic electromagnetic forces. If you take two simple magnets and place them together at opposite poles, they cling to each other. Flip one and you can't make them touch. Very powerful forces, indeed!

So, how do we see them? Each atom puts out photons of a distinct frequency (think color) in our visible light range that our brain can detect and smear into an image. It then creates a video, framing the images at a fast enough rate that we see motion and consider that to be our reality. Real enough to work for us in our daily lives, but only because we allow our brain to cherry-pick from all the outside stimuli we are bombarded with, to create a nice reality while ignoring all those beyond our consciousness that

Quantum Brain

we also bump into but can live without knowledge of. We can have a nice life without ever worrying about the various cosmic particles that constantly pass through us or the changes in the many magnetic fields that flutter through our own body's magnetic fields, all detected by the quantum functions in our brain but overridden by the reality functioning.

Does this mean we are missing something that we might need in order to live the full life we hope and strive for in our real world? Yes, and it's there for the taking if we tune into our quantum brain functioning, that is, Rhoality.

Access to this quantum state (Rho) is not hard to achieve but the brain has to be in the right mindset. It is wired by design to do its best when it believes that is fully informed about the nature and state of its own body and can analyze quickly and accurately the changes in its environment that the incoming stimuli provide. Not easy in a world that creates so much more of these beyond-sensory stimuli than ever before. They keep us in a constant state of anxiety about our safety and security, what we term our survival state. Even small worries keep us there.

Event Wave Function EWF

The nature of the quantum collapse of waves into particles we call matter (see Table 1) has been long known to science. Einstein called parts of quantum science spooky action at a distance. Although widely acknowledged as true physics, it really is metaphysics, so how it works has been ignored in favor of learning how to use it. Early experiments to at least corral it in resulted in even more magic, such as defining just what collapses, which actually is the wave function, another physics term. It has to do with the wave nature of all particles and their characteristic probabilities. But the nature of experiments is such that they have results that can't be pinned down to a single property, like spin or location. They are described in terms of the upper-level physics (that enables reality) that rests atop the quantum physics (that enables Rhoality). This creates a strange being called the event wave function (EWF) to handle the collapse of the experiment results from a

Quantum Brain

cloud of possibilities to a single result. Niels Bohr, an early pioneer in the quantum nature of atoms, described the EWFs as *hovering* around the experiment, then collapsing to a result upon being observed.

It gets stranger. Where do these EWFs come from? Event Collapse Theory (James Circe, Power of the Quantum Mind) describes them as originating in the conscious mind whenever a future event or situation is envisioned. There the progress of the EFW is maintained and updated until the event occurs, the originator nulls it or reality changes enough to make it impossible. Actually, it would seem that the only reason for the initial introduction of EWF collapses in science is to give the conscious mind the power to direct the future.

Event collapses are the mechanism that turns the quantum world into our reality. Our universe hands us a stack of building blocks that can form a large number of shapes but not infinite. As we build the structure, each block placement depends on how we did the previous ones. The event collapse is the result of the

Rhoality Guide to Wellness

decision of which block goes on next and how does it conform to our vision of the final product. Success occurs when the probability is increased significantly above all other possibilities.

Belief

As we have seen, the brain can only be at peak performance when belief is present. It usually comes from smoking-gun proof or when our rationality overcomes the doubts that creep in along the way.

If you are willing to accept the possibility of a quantum brain that senses things that we are never consciously aware of, analyzes this new data in light of how our life is situated at the moment, determines the best actions for us to take to maximize the probability of our getting what we want (or think we want), considers the emotional impact of the choices before selecting one, then publishes the final action

Quantum Brain

effect in whatever way one human body can interface with others in order to make them be a help to us, then you don't need to go further into quantum science to achieve the necessary belief.

Acceptance isn't belief, but it will allow us to develop it as the magic of Rhoality becomes clearer. Nagging doubts are a real hindrance to success and must be overcome with knowledge and some understanding. Even if you have faith, you can still harbor doubts. When the doubts are gone, you have belief.

Magic is defined as a hidden cause. Miracles are when we can see only the effect and believe there is no cause. Belief in an afterlife is more acceptance than certainty. Claiming that you don't believe something exists is not the same as believing that it doesn't.

Rhoality was not meant to be fully understood by the human mind any more than quantum physics was. For some reason, mankind was allowed to evolve its intelligence and intellectual achievements to the point that we can prove it

Rhoality Guide to Wellness

works, but not how. When we wonder why Rhoality wasn't discovered before now, we have only to point to the century that classical science grew to its current peak of understanding without invoking the metascience below it. That has changed. Classical science has now proven the undeniable possibility of Rhoality, never before done. A new generation, reared on quantum thinking, will be free to pursue the new truths about our existence without having to overcome the barrier of "Get real!".

The Rho State

A major but largely unused feature of our brain is the quantum computing power that resides inside cells and within the brain energy field. Classical psychology defines the brain states that go from the lowest brain wave frequency (Delta) during sleep to the highest (Gamma) during high anxiety. The quantum brain state (Rho) is physically less definable and centers

Quantum Brain

around the transition from the middle reality mind state Alpha (daydreams) to Theta (subconscious). This is where our conscious and subconscious minds meet. This state handles the quantum connection to the brain space energy field (the Rho field) and handshakes with the brain through its magnetic field and quantum entanglement. This makes the Rho field data accessible to our conscious mind.

Everything is simply probabilities until observed by a consciousness.

The Rho State gives rise to reality and provides the brain with the coherence and calmness that it needs to function optimally. This allows it to correctly comprehend the health data from all the cells and organs of the body. A calm coherent brain can fend off all outside invaders and repair minor physical damage and most importantly, will keep the brain from creating the miscues that are so self-destructive. The path to the Rho state is the Entrex process.

In summary, having our mind in the Rho state enables Rhoality and provides the brain the

Rhoality Guide to Wellness

coherence and calmness that it needs to function optimally. This allows it to correctly comprehend the health state of all the cells and organs of the body. A calm, coherent brain can fend off all outside invaders and repair minor physical damage. Most importantly, it will not create brain miscues.

The Rhoality Process

In our everyday world, believing our own eyes serves us well. That is, until it doesn't.

What is Rhoality and how does it work? Rhoality is the experience of the brain's quantum workings. To understand it, one must first understand reality, because one is truth and the other a take-off of that truth. Surprising to most of us, science has now proven that our daily experience we call reality is a cartoon-like sequence of events in our daily experience that pretend to be true.

Quantum Brain

Rhoality begins deep within our being, down inside the quantum workings of brain matter and energy that rule our existence. It is based on the quantum Rho state of the mind, using the basic forces that created our universe, the core of the science that had to be simplified so that we could understand our own reality. For most of human history, this false narrative on ourselves has worked well as we used it to conquer first nature, then disease, then ourselves.

Yes, our brains are quantum machines, and it is this feature of Rhoality that makes everything in reality work for us and mostly work well. But even our brains turn against us when mistreated. There are countless books on how to keep the physical body fit but fewer user manuals on how to keep our brain happy. However mental health is a prerequisite to physical health. We can draw on vast physical reserves to keep us fighting the daily battles of life but the lack of replenishment of these resources eventually causes disease and malfunctions in the body and brings us down.

Rhoality Guide to Wellness

Rhoality outlines a simple process to permit the brain to tend to our physical needs and allows us to live at a sustainable level that lets us be the best we can be.

Rhoality is what makes our reality possible. It works as a powerful, almost imperceptible, facility that takes advantage of the amazing quantum computer in all of us. It tries to stay hidden so as not to muddle our take on our daily lives, what we mistake for the truth of reality. Based on a balanced, coherent mind, it tries to maintain our health, improve our relationship with others, and have a long, safe, and happy life. All it asks of us is to be treated with respect; that is, kept free of chronic anxiety.

Rhoality vs Reality

Reality is the brain's take on what is in its environment. Rhoality is the full experience of the quantum connection to reality. Reality is presented to us by images in the mind that let us live through time in a video. Rhoality is

Quantum Brain

hidden in the space inside and between the atoms in the brain (Rho Space) and must have its results turned into reality before we can comprehend its effects and allow the conscious mind to create what we think of as awareness.

Our reality isn't made aware of what is happening inside the quantum mind area but the brain is aware of many things that are not brought into focus long enough to register in our memory as a true awareness, such as fleeting images or minor sensory stimuli. If one's mind is busy thinking of something else, the unaware things won't register even as brainwave fluctuations. Thus, any quantum action in the brain is of such a short impact duration that it doesn't register or disturb the wave output.

Rhoality is combining the reality of the senses with the unaware stimuli impacting the brain to create a full slate of responses, considering all stimuli, not just the five senses.

Rhoality was designed to provide the framework for a balanced life with a quiet faith in the

Rhoality Guide to Wellness

future. It is meant to be the truth and provide a constant set of data focus. Reality is designed to create emotion.

Being part of a group is important. If you don't feel like you belong, you can't ever find esteem.

Emotions

We understand when people react due to an emotional stimulus from whatever we just said – anger, fear, sorrow, despair. When someone behaves this way, they are invoking a powerful control weapon against us. The judicious use of emotional reaction is a learned art form and many people have analyzed and practiced it. The control process starts with a quick facial display to reinforce your fear of their planning an irrational action. They know that allowing it to linger can quickly reinforce our resistance, so must be chopped quickly. You can see them regaining control of themselves and thinking clearly again, but the atmosphere says that they could be pushed easily back into the emotional reaction if you don't back off.

All emotions can confuse the mind and prevent rational thought, even gratitude (although more likely just the absence of emotion). That is why the brain saves their use until the end to finalize the decision.

We need be concerned with only events that are created in our minds that result in a decision on the collapse of its EWF. Occurrences that we observe but have no emotion attached may have an EWF themselves through another consciousness. When we first become cognizant of a potential future event, if we pull up an emotion for it, an EWF is created and collapsed for it in our reality as we decide on one.

Deep emotions often evolve into life's passions. When you allow one to take over, you shut out all other balancing actions involved that your brain could make for you.

Rhoality Guide to Wellness

Rhoality and the Brain

Recall that we previously discussed that what your eyes see is a continuous stream of gillions of tiny light packets, each in the form of a cloud of possibilities as to what is inside. The brain has to select one of the possibilities from each packet, then smear them together into our reality.

The brain has no external constraints on which probability it chooses, and thus uses its own internal data; that is emotions, morality, comfort, desires, etc, to select one. It may not even be the most probable one. It uses this quantum computing program, that is, the Rho Matrix, to access data stored inside the brain in Rho Space, to increase the odds that favor what the brain thinks is most desired for its body. It gets that desire from the envisioning that we do. That comes from daydreams, hopes, fears, or decided-on action, that the mind comes up with.

Quantum Brain

ERN – Error Related Negativity

Error related negativity (ERN) is an auto error correction by the brain. It is a component of an event-related potential (ERP) that occurs in conjunction with the extended or mental stimulus after an error, often a wrong choice made by the brain. This double response is a measurable and well-documented reality event. Even though the consciousness can be unaware of the error, any emotion can overwrite the first subconscious reaction. This happens in time for the consciousness to correct the error before it causes a response to reach its destination.

Any ERN can be the result of the Rho Matrix presenting data to the brain causing it to rethink what it wants to do. Science says the consciousness is never aware that the change is being corrected. So, it looks like a standard process. It is often considered an error but is more likely to be just more detail to make the event collapse decision. This is supported by the fact that the conscious mind handles 2000 bits

Rhoality Guide to Wellness

per second but the subconscious processes 400 billion. Sometimes the conscious mind gets ahead of the Rho Matrix input and chooses the wrong option. It then must correct its directions to the muscles before they complete the action command. Science supports ERN in our system.

This book is the follow-on guide to the previous work in the Rhoality series: *Power of the Quantum Mind, Passion Spent*, and *The Very Man.* Thus, most of the subjects and some sections are taken directly from them, abridged, and updated. A full copy of the Triverity description is reproduced here in Appendix C. These are the ideas that have formed the basis of the results from research, but current information that doesn't directly affect belief or the process of Rhoality living are moved to the appendices or omitted entirely. Further details can be found in Circe's *A Walk with the Shadows*, which is the trilogy of the above-mentioned books.

Quantum Brain

It is meant to serve as a user's manual for anyone investigating or delving deeper into the scientific truth of Rhoality.

Five

Rho Visions

Rho Visions

Introduction

At this point, the reader should have had enough positive experiences with Entrex to have created a high level of trust in the Rhoality functioning of the brain. This will suffice to allow for access to the seemingly magical help we can expect it to provide.

Rho Matrix processes live and die by the power of probabilities because that's what drives the universe. We all have a level of acceptable odds that allows us to proceed down a course of action with a certain amount of confidence.

Let's turn from being concerned with proving the truth of the science of existence to using what we have found true to make our remaining time here on earth to be the best it can be. If our understanding of the science is deep enough to allow belief in the science behind Rhoality, then it has accomplished its purpose.

Rhoality Guide to Wellness

Our understanding of how the Rhoality process works determines the actions in life that we choose. It also lets us avoid false stimuli and feelings that would draw us away from our guided path and help us adjust when we drift off it.

Envisioning

We have discussed how positive thinking coupled with belief can improve our chances of getting more success in life. We follow a simple heads-up process of staying aware and focusing on what our brains are saying to us to prevent an unbalanced mind from turning from a close friend into a very powerful enemy. If we stopped there and practiced this disciplined life, we would realize almost all those benefits.

But the creators went much further for us in their design. They have incorporated a quantum computer into our brains that not only can analyze the data made available by our five senses but also the beyond-sensory stimuli that

Rho Visions

bombard us even beyond instinct and intuition. This facility can access the almost infinite amount of information stored up through the millennia that brains have been on earth. The data is stored in the quantum recesses of the brain and is detectable enough to give our brain an almost perfect prediction capability into events that we face. Coupled with the rule of quantum collapse by observers, it creates a near-magical path for us to influence the future to our own benefit. The combination of a coherent brain, an awareness in its being on our side and willing and able to do us good beyond our understanding, our practice of living in the Rhoality state, our ability to create and pronounce clear and realistic goals and, perhaps most important, our belief that by setting this process in motion, we will guide our own futures, gives us that power.

Sometimes awareness and reality seem to be close to the same thing. Awareness is the result of stimuli being brought to the consciousness. Reality is the video at the end of the process of interpreting and analyzing the changes. By the

Rhoality Guide to Wellness

time the brain has put together a new frame for the video, all decisions concerning the event and new situation resulting from it have been made.

Since the result of this cloud of possibilities we call an event is also created by an observation, that means that the observer can help determine the nature of the collapse. But only if it is envisioned in a clear enough fashion that the Rho Matrix can determine the vast number of events that have to occur along the way. This is called the event path and the final goal is called the end event.

We do this by envisioning the events as we wish them to happen. When we follow the process that invokes the Rho feature of the brain, we call that a Rho Vision

Rho Vision Plays Out

Recall that we have described how the world we see and sense, what we call reality, is simply a video placed in our minds. The quantum world,

Rho Visions

the world of truth, underlies and determines how our daily happenings play out for us.

As waves are collapsed into particles in the lower world so are events in reality collapsed by the brain processing Rho visions. As we decide, so it goes. We need to define how this could be scientifically possible or our acceptance will never turn to belief. We will explore the process that the mind has in the Rho matrix and how it can take its knowledge of the past, present, and future and use it to predict how our action of observation can collapse the wave function of future events to our benefit.

Proper envisioning will increase the end event probability. Sometimes, the more detail, the better. At other times, the specifics of an event simply restrict the possibilities that may help things turn out better. In any case, spending the time and thought to get things right and clear in your mind is necessary. This includes deciding the emotional input and output that pleases you in the long run. Remember, envisioning bad things gives them life.

Rhoality Guide to Wellness

Rho Events

What are these events we're talking about? We think of them as a reality view shown to us through our eyes that is different from the previous view. Since the changes are usually small, we don't pay much attention to them. Clouds drift by without etching their motion in our memory. If they suddenly turn gray, we pull up a memory of dark clouds and feel the emotion that we previously attached to them. If alarming enough, we have a decision to make on how to react.

Lots of things happen to us. Some we can sense through the five senses and either use or reject and some that we can only detect but never become consciously aware of. To be meaningful to the Rho Matrix, we define an event as a change in a situation that the brain recognizes as being salient to our life. Refer to Table 2.

Rho Visions

Table 2. Rho Event Terms

Situation	How your mind sees the sequence of states of a narrow mind view.
Occurrence	A change in reality.
Event Wave Function	EWF: the wave function associated with an envisioned event.
Event Collapse	A selection of one of the probabilities in the event cloud.

External events change the probabilities of the various path events leading to our envisioned end event. The Rho Matrix is continually reanalyzing stimuli to get new probabilities for each event in each path. Every time it changes reality, that change is called an occurrence. For example, if the creek rises, the path to the other side may have to also change. So, limits count here – rises how much? As it continues to rise, the probability of any given event on each path decreases nearer to zero.

We can think of path event collapse as what your consciousness would do if it had awareness of all the possible events in the path. The brain has to define the major steps on the path as decision points that when some limit is hit, the path must also change.

A Good Process

The Rho Matrix has identified and continually redefines many path events that must be successfully gained to get a successful end event. It combines what is possible with what we desire to create the visioning.

Envisioning is giving substance to an imagined event. But envisioned events are more complicated than the simple happenings we are used to. They arise when an emotion is applied to a situation in our reality (see Table

Rho Visions

2). The situation is the total of all the parts that make up the state of reality at any given moment. If it is a present situation, it closely mirrors the reality video that our mind continually presents to us. If it is one that could occur in the future, it is created by our imagination.

A successful event would then be the basis for the brain's final selection of a path. For instance, as you're watching someone open presents, you envision them opening yours and getting a big smile on their faces. When they first handle it with a smile, it ups the anticipation. This event `allows you to attach a pleasure emotion to the memory even as you anticipate a more positive one later on. You then watch as they fumble with over-taped wrapping. The smile fades and the event turns into a bump that stays with you and lessens the pleasure you get when you finally see a smile again. The machinery at the factory that wrapped it for you allowed no foreknowledge of this negative event so your brain had little prior reason to cause it to take it into consideration.

The small negative effects showed up only in the path's probability value, buried among others and obviously not significant enough to undo the deal. Indeed, even someone watching the unwrapping would have no indication of the mind state of the present receiver at the end event moment. The faded smile may have been tiredness or some unrelated unpleasant memory from the past clouding their enjoyment.

However, the big smile then happens, just as you had envisioned, slightly subdued by the path events that you couldn't possibly have anticipated and tried to alter. You will have to make allowances for unexpected bumps (events that for emotional reasons are less acceptable) whichever way you envision.

Bumps that can't be overcome are those like the death of a participant, physical objects like rockslides interfering, and doubts on your end.

Rho Visions

Even a low probability can emotionally crash things.

The cosmos has stored knowledge of how previous observers changed the physical world, so knows how your interaction with it would possibly work out for you. The Rho Matrix runs every possibility through your brain for it to determine which emotions are generated for each possible set of events. The conscious brain rejects the ones that cause mental pain above a certain threshold and goes with the ones that offer the highest pleasure combined with the greatest probability of being successful. Chances are least for ones that contain emotional pain. You may want to take the consequences of a bad move but survive and acquire the most learning from the event. The Rho Matrix uses your history of envisioning and daydreaming in its calculation of probabilities for the correct path to a desired end.

The Rho Matrix was designed to automatically give your consciousness a list of possible event paths (sometimes denoted in science as a cloud

Rhoality Guide to Wellness

and in mystics as an intention) to get what your envisioning wants to make happen, with the probability of success for each one attached. Keep in mind here that our brain orchestrates our reality by merging what we perceive as our current state of things (situation) with information from the past, looking toward the future. The events that require decisions are the ones that our brain is allowed to work with.

Event selection decisions are based on logical goals over a logical path and set in motion by logical actions. The brain tends to the health business of the body while the Rho Matrix sets up the necessary workings to guide us to the desired final event. It may be true at this point to describe the connection as an entangled quantum computer that drives how our reality plays out.

How do you reconcile the quiet positive feeling about the future with the thought of jumping on a problem early and nipping it in the bud? No problem there. Early fix is very desirable. Just don't get so involved in the process that

Rho Visions

the tension that it inserts becomes chronic. Early deterrent is a way of dampening anxiety.

Envisions that involve another consciousness are more straightforward and perhaps more powerful but can cause problems to others. If you simply want a loved one to feel good about themselves, your choice of an event that you think would do the trick is itself tricky. The chance of a completely successful path could be complicated, and that particular end event may not be the best way to go since things change that you are not aware of.

Situation

Looking ahead at where we want to end up usually results in envisioning a situation rather than a single event. It's a way of ensuring that the events involved give the total picture of the end event. But it has its own problems, being tricky as well as risky. Bumps can occur much more easily, making the overall action bad in hidden ways. A well-thought-out set of events allows us to become coherent and could prevent some of the bumps or at least make them detectable, giving a more guided approach to the end event.

A situation can be defined as how your mind alters its perception of the sequence of states of a narrow mind view. It is a constantly changing view of our world. A reality event is the application of an emotion to a new situation or to the result of an occurrence. Stimuli have to individually collapse together into an event which then determines the current situation.

You consciously analyze the new situation and decide on a reaction (grab an umbrella, perhaps). That situation is stored and becomes the new current situation when you next check out the clouds. Many unrelated things have happened meanwhile but none are likely to be pertinent to the end event of your getting soaked or blown away even if you could change the weather, which isn't realistic.

Rho Visions

Event wave function collapses are different from simple photon quantum collapses. Once any EWF is created, the possible paths are defined by the Rho Matrix.

The Rho matrix plays out the path to the end event, so it knows the likelihood of how they end. It analyzes the event probabilities but doesn't collapse events right away. It presents them as data comprehensible by the brain, which then plays out each possible path, considering the emotional impact. If it sees a bump, it goes on to the next probable path and so on until it finds one that doesn't lead to an unacceptable bump. The Rho Matrix then accepts the brain-selected data to alter the current situation for the next stimulus.

The process can be quantified by following its progress. Before the stimuli start things off, a desired occurrence (a change in the current situation such as the your boss or a client looking more favorably toward your presentation) is needed.

Rhoality Guide to Wellness

ERN Use in Rhoality Events.

When a spot in the brain activates due to an external stimulus, that doesn't necessarily indicate that part of the brain is analyzing, storing, or responding to the stimulus. That feature in the brain is powering up as a communication function to alert the quantum function in the brain, the Rho Matrix, and handshakes with it for the correct response. Indeed, the brain quickly selects and transmits a response. But, as discussed previously, if the final answer is different, it quickly retransmits the new answer to overwrite the first one using an ERN.

Rho Visions

Time Considerations

The longer the envision is held in your mind, the deeper it will be ingrained. Once there, no further action is required by you, only allowing the quiet faith in the future to do its thing. However, if things change along the way, you may not want the end event to remain the same and the envisioning will have to be repeated with the new information. Indeed, leaving the envision to default on its own may result in undefined results. If something included in your envisioning happens in an adverse way whether it was due to your unbalance or not, you will have to consider the possibility that you were involved. Better to tidy up loose ends.

Give your brain time to do its housework to make a clear connection to the Rho Matrix. Shut your eyes, open your ears, and relax your mind so that it doesn't negate the Entrex action. Let go of the Entrex muscles and savor the feeling of anxiety loss through free movements. Think

Rhoality Guide to Wellness

positive thoughts. Smile, laugh, feel gratitude for your situation and your lack of pain. Bring your desired end of the situation to mind and ponder the consequence of its success. If you're still smiling, bring to mind the individual events that might lead to the end event. Don't overly consider the bumps that may exist in the path. When the Rho Matrix creates the possible paths, it allows the brain to reject any bumps at that time. Some of them that may seem unacceptable at the envision time may be necessary or even desirable as the end event nears. In any case, if your brain has been wired to not go toward any of them, they won't affect the highest probability paths much. This is due to the fact that the value, that is the intensity, of the bump action has already been factored into the probability for the path.

As for the time from the envision to the end, the event has to be far enough away for small changes in the current situation to work smoothly. Very short changes are hard to make work. Too far away in time results in too many bumps in the paths as external things change.

Rho Visions

Your brain, in cahoots with the Rho Matrix, doesn't depend on your envisioning all the time. It knows through your choices, mostly through your selection of emotions, how you want an end event to finish. This is your personal guardian. Trying to understand how the guardian does things leads back to the Rho Matrix being there for the analysis.

The end event isn't fully determined at envisioning. It is the result of success in all the path events, collapsing to create a final state at end event time.

Other observers may see it going your way and try to intervene. No way to stop that. We have to just keep overwriting it. Most end events won't have a competing vision, but if so, could be a race to the finish.

Your envisioning won't perform far-off miracles like saving the Titanic from sinking to keep you from drowning, but it could steer you away from traveling.

Six

How to Use Rhoality

How to use Rhoality

An Effective Rho Vision

To make the Rho Vision most effective, there are two necessary steps, one physical, and one mental. The physical is Entrex, which takes the mind to the Rho state and clears a pathway for the Rho Matrix. The mental step is the mind itself which goes to the theta/alpha reality state and settles down into the Rho state.

An effective envisioning must be focused and thought out and not overly emotional so as to seem permanent and directed at somebody in a timely manner. It will require objectives that are well-defined. Envisioning peace on earth is a noble goal, but the events involved are too numerous to be fathomed, let alone defined as individual specific actions and are unlikely to have a significant impact. Trying to make a change in a non-sentient object is a waste of time unless you are physically doing the altering.

Emotional values attached to the envision serve a purpose but are double-edged swords. On the positive side, they add energy and purpose to

Rhoality Guide to Wellness

the end event. On the downside, they often override a logical, well-thought-out goal.

If your envision is to be offered a job, it is better to aim your vision to have the decision-making people pleased with you to the point they want you to have the job. Then, if the job slot disappears, you still reap the benefit of the envisioning, which will set the stage for the net try.

As previously discussed, the EWF created at the start contains an impossibly large number of possibilities to make any sense, and the farther away it is in time, the harder that task is. As time passes, it all becomes clearer to our mind as the possibilities become fewer.

We often wish for things that later don't come about. Wishful thinking, daydreams, romantic yearnings, imagined journeys or experiences, all are desired end events to a string of lesser intermediate happenings. We don't place a high probability on their reality or else we could call them a plan.

How to use Rhoality

An example: You want to buy something but someone in line ahead of you is admiring it. You see yourself walking out the door with it, but they ask the price and smile. You refocus on your envision and watch as they put it down and walk away.

It's tempting to consider an isolated event like this as a coincidence, but when your belief is reinforced by an extraordinary number of successes, you stop harboring doubts.

In this example your gain is someone else's loss, albeit on a small scale here. In more dire situations, they are both magnified.

As an aside, if you are the first to observe the result of an event, your perception becomes reality for anyone who looks later in the same way. This ties in with being a guardian for someone else to help them accomplish their own vision. Keep at it.

Rhoality Guide to Wellness

Focus

Constant focusing on the end event helps collapse the intermediate events that make up the path. It is similar to focusing energy by the brain for healing in meditation. Some other mental observers could be changing things along the way. It would work for you to have other observers working on your vision also. Tests have shown that mentally envisioning learning to play the piano rewires the brain the same way as actual practice, so the mind can accomplish that. Note that the second observer is forced to your result only if they observe it in the same way.

It takes a lot of concentration, training, and relief to guide a vision to success, so it's best to stay in the Rho state and trust. The daily results of our efforts are disease prevention and healing of the mind as well as having many more hours around pleasant people.

How to use Rhoality

Imagination

We usually daydream about a sort of wistful distant future, something that we suspect is beyond us, then wait to see what happens. Meanwhile, we turn back to the reality of daily life and are somewhat surprised when it turns out right.

If it is important enough to us, we usually try to come up with a reality plan that could reasonably get us there. This requires a sequence of successful actions on our part that moves things along. When one of these interim events goes wrong, we abandon all hope and look for a more possible but usually less rewarding outcome. The disappointment and other emotional downs unbalance our brains, preventing a well-thought-out and directed alternative path to the desired end event. We settle for less by turning to a plan that is riskier and has a more expensive, in terms of expended resources, set of events to get back on the original path. Either way, our lack of belief in the

Rhoality Guide to Wellness

future short-circuits our ability to make things happen as we want.

The Rho Vision is a way to achieve the goal by allowing our Rho Matrix to guide the events using its awesome quantum power of predictability and quantum entanglement, with the information that other peoples' brains also use to determine the probabilities that we all factor into our decision making.

The more ardent we are for our path, the more our Rho Matrix can skew other paths to increase our probability of success. As has been said, the world steps aside for someone who knows where they are going.

Rho Visions are driven by perfect clarity of the goal and ardent belief in success. The clarity comes from the brain coming up with a desired end event free from distraction and doubt, along with saying it out loud, at least to oneself. The belief starts with knowledge of how quantum science not only allows the magic of quantum physics to make Rho Vision power possible but could be the original intent.

How to use Rhoality

A Rho Vision is different from wishful thinking in its focus and belief.

When you picture in your mind an event in the future (image or video), if your subconscious mind has been programmed by a previous stimulus happening, it will dig out from memory the emotion that you gave it when it was stored, then attach the old feelings to the new vision. These events often fade from memory unless the emotion is powerful.

This process gives our imagination lots of power since it creates the EWF that results in the specific events envisioned. The imagined event should be described in as much detail as is known. If you want the basketball to go through the hoop, imagine it doing that so that the brain knows specifically what the end event looks like so it can guide your muscles to make it happen. If you imagine a situation, say that we win the game, the definition of win could mean something besides just a higher score. It may be undetermined or unrecognizable since winning could be taken to mean something such as just getting through the game without a fistfight.

Rhoality Guide to Wellness

Indeed, there are many possible paths to many end events. The event wave function is scattered over many observers and their paths to success are packed at the top of the list. There is no obvious way for the brain to select one. Which events will have any certain effect on the end event is fuzzy.

And, this is important, remember that there must be belief that it will work as envisioned.

The collapse of an event by an observer is based on the wave function created at envisioning time. The imagination drives all future event collapses. Part of it is what we think we should see, so our imagination drives our next version of reality. Our brain allows us to display an image that lets us imagine the next image to be similar or slightly altered by movement or external changes to the object.

Since our imagination also creates future events that we don't want in our path, we need to continually adjust the EWF from the brain, usually when we have new info that changes our

How to use Rhoality

perception of what the end event will or should be.

It's tempting to use Rhoality to get back at someone for a transgression. The decision to reject making threats is a major factor in any confrontation decision but accepting a path with one in it is sufficient to unbalance any brain. On the other hand, if the end event of a search were to be a new heart for your child, you could likely not reject the use of threats to win. Any dire situation like that is a challenge for us but need not be. Returning to Rhoality state is always the best bet for success.

Rhoality Guide to Wellness

Table 3. Key Elements of Rhoality

1. Whatever you give your time to prospers and grows. Focusing on positive things draws help from inside and outside and leaves less time for entertaining negatives.

2. At birth, we have all the physical tools in place we will ever have. Most of the important decisions in our life have already been made, taken from our ancestral DNA and the nutrition and environment our parents provide.

3. Your brain is on your side. It cares only about your survival in the best possible manner. Only the insertion of emotion can lead it down a different path.

4. The brain can maintain health for the body and cure all internally derived ailments. These include all diseases and malfunctions that aren't a result of physical damage, inheritance, or our

How to use Rhoality

body being packed with chemicals.

5. The brain cannot do its job effectively unless balanced and coherent. It tries to return to a calm state (the Rho state) when it completes a fight-or-flight survival.

6. A conscious mind relaxation process called Entrex can return the brain to the coherent Rho state and prevent brain miscues like insomnia, constipation, muscle cramps, tension headaches, and possibly all auto-immune dysfunctions. These messages are signals that an Entrex is needed and are the initial stimuli that precede brain miscues.

7. The ultimate life process is achieved through a calm, well-developed brain process called Rhoality. It leads to the absence of chronic brain miscues.

8. The quantum functioning of the brain,

called the Rho Matrix, uses its quantum computing power and a connection with the information stored in the brain energy fields to predict the most likely and efficacious paths for us when decisions need to be made. It makes this data available to the reality functioning of the brain in a list, referred to in the quantum world as a cloud.

9. Like in the quantum world, events exist as a cloud of probabilities until they are observed by a consciousness. The brain applies emotion to the cloud created by the Rho Matrix to decide on the best path to the end event. They are then collapsed (selected) into a single state in reality. In this manner, Rhoality allows us to influence this decision in our favor by raising the odds for what we want.

How to use Rhoality

10. We focus our daily (and eventual) life goals into a process called Rho Vision. It allows us to determine the path to the end event using an imagination process to get the event to turn out like we wish it to. One example of envisioning is daydreaming. When the vision is turned into intention with belief it becomes a Rho Vision.

Seven

Rhoality Life Flow

Rhoality Life Flow

Rho Life Flow

In our desire for a full life, we would like to be able to maximize our physical pleasures while remaining safe and secure and still have all the other mental positives such as achievement, esteem, praise from others, health, feeling good, free from pain. etc. Obviously, as hard as we might try, none of us are able to maximize all these. Most events are controlled by nature or other people, who obviously add negatives. We trade some of our wealth (money, things, time, energy, and intellectual assets) to gain things we want from others.

If we were wise enough, we could maximize our net input by not squandering this bartering by a lack of savvy or simple greed or overreaching. The closest we can get to that wisdom is knowing ourselves - our physical and mental limits and what we really want and how we should value each asset or opportunity.

Rhoality Guide to Wellness

Our life flow can be predefined for us as being the events that make up a path to be the best we can be. It defines the purpose in life that enables our decision-making guide. We will use flow to outline a smooth course of events that gives us the best path to the last end event of our lives.

We could create a smoother flow in our life by choreographing events that could get the most value in return each time we strike a deal with our inner self. If we were to plot a chart of the events in our life over time as to whether that day or even individual occurrences in each day, added to our feelings of negative or positive in relation to how we felt at the end of our previous day, we would see a wavy line as we sense the emotional ups and downs of each action.

If we are succeeding in achieving our life goals, the curve is smoother and unerringly trends upwards as our career savvy and asset worth increase over time. A spike upward on the graph would indicate an overreach that somehow turned out good. A downward spike could show that we lost our risky bet and had to start again from a lower level. But be aware. The good feeling from an upward spike is small compared to the loss from a downward one.

Our objective, when we can shelf the cares of the world and enjoy looking back, is to be glad of our accomplishments – our relationship with family and friends; good health over many years; no regrets from moral decisions; the feeling that we maximized our potential well. But remember, you will not end up higher than your ending Rho potential no matter how hard-working, lucky or adventurous you are.

Plotting a Flow Line

To plot the flow of your life, start with a list of the events as they occurred in time or are certain to occur, like the death of an aging parent. Be as specific as possible. Mark each one with a minus if it was negative or a plus if it was

Rhoality Guide to Wellness

positive. Start a graph with the x-axis (horizontal) as time in your life from birth to 100 years. Make the y-axis the relative positive (up) and negative (down) measure of satisfaction level, however you measure that in your life. Put a dot near the down left corner of the graph as a starting point. All further dots will be relative to the one just before it in time.

Connect all the dots into a line. It should look like an irregular wavy sine type of wave as it shows the high and low points interspersed. If there is too much variation in the distance between peaks (large time span between positive and negative), fill in the list with neglected events, even minor ones.

A frequency will start forming. The more peaks per inch, the greater the frequency and the higher the energy level you live with. Your body energy levels will be determined by it. Having a constant frequency in your flow line will create a corresponding resonance that reacts to other people. It is best to try for a constant level throughout life.

Rhoality Life Flow

The trick is to not create unnecessary spikes in either up or down direction. Our objective of a healthy life that enables the possible pleasures we are gifted can be achieved without either. We gain enough experience along the way to know deep inside when the odds of a successful venture are enough against us that the resulting anxiety is likely to keep our brains confused and lower the odds considerably. We need to resist the temptation of bowing to gold fever or greed and lower our input and expectations of the return to stay below that level. This gives us the added health benefit of maximizing the brain's time in a balanced, coherent state.

Emotions are attached to occurrences (and situations) to turn them into events. All emotions have shadows, even the pleasant ones. All spikes decohere the brain and can result in chronic brain miscues but emotional ones are the most impactful. You should plan to level the spike out near where it started.

Rhoality Guide to Wellness

Be brave enough to pencil in the line you think you can follow. Include obvious spikes like graduations, income bumps, partnering with someone else, investment payoffs, retirement, etc. You can imagine and put in the events that comprise the path along the way at a time you think you might be there. Be as honest as you can about not only your capabilities but also your determination to resist long stretches of being easy on yourself, such as thrill-seeking or devil-may-care risk taking. You may not be able to make your industry your entertainment, like the famous ant, but you can stay within the limits you set for yourself. By looking at the chart up to the present, you gain an idea of how the future might look for you.

After you get the line from your birth to the present, expand it in a line to the 100-year mark. It will go through and be defined by the most significant point yet to come, the best you can be from a lifetime of trying. This part of the line will be your near future life flow line. It will be your first estimate of the progress you need to make to reach your old age goal. It is based

Rhoality Life Flow

on what you find an acceptable use of your life to live it fully and will be adjusted periodically as you become aware of how much more potential you actually have. Until you fill it with real data, you will use it in making decisions on how much resource you can contribute to any envisioned end event.

Risking resources that puts your anxiety level above the line will leave you in danger of decohering your brain with worry and uncertainty about the result just when you have to make a clear and well thought out decision. Lowering expectations by lowering the risk keeps the mind clear and adds to the probability that the end event will be successful. Little is lost in doing this and it leaves the next step up also more doable. As long as you follow the line, you will reach the desired end point with few downward spikes.

One thing must be brought out here – paths that are interesting and useful but really don't belong in the flow line, for example, a childhood dream of learning to speak foreign languages, can be a positive event but doesn't necessarily lay down the base for the next flow level. Wasted resources, maybe, but the positive here, besides the encouragement of a success, is the result of a failure, whether through lack of ability, not enough interest to pay attention, or simply moving on to another interest, allows you to not waste further resources in tidying up the fraying ends. A two-edged sword, to be sure, but knowing that there is an anxiety-free exit allows you to be OK with accepting the challenge, knowing it won't drag you down if it doesn't play out right. Good learning experience, at the least. Sadder but wiser.

Flow Analysis

When you do a plot, hopefully, it will look like a gently rising wavy line. The location of each point can be estimated by the feeling of an inner nervousness or elation when the action is envisioned. The points that are a consequence of failure rise in youth due to shortened recovery time but are lessened due to

Rhoality Life Flow

acceptance of abilities as aging brings wisdom to expectations.

We will need all the physical resources we acquire at birth to create our life structure from then on. We are molded less and less by others as we take more and more responsibility for our own future. These resources dictate a limit on the process toward the structure and we would waste resources by aiming for goals that require capabilities that are beyond what is possible. The highest level we can obtain is by following the path provided by Rhoality, using a quiet confidence to guide us. Instead of addressing stimuli with drastic action, we let things play out and subtlty guide them. The rule for this is: *I may not ever be the best but I will try to be the best I can be.*

As well as physical, you have all the mental tools, including brain function and capability that you are ever going to have. After that, life is learning how to use the tools and sharpen them. This is managed by your caregivers until you hit life flow onset, where you start making your own decisions. Society will start its pounding process directly on you instead of allowing your internal caregiver to see to the task.

Facility strength

Your facility strength begins with your capabilities when you become able to make life decisions on your own. At that moment is the start of your near future life flow, or the smooth process of growing from life's experiences. From that day on, it becomes important to know your capabilities, not only so you can correctly select directions like careers, interests, etc., but also, and more important for us, it allows you to know more about what the accepted level of anxiety you can create for yourself by how you decide to approach the actions you take. The desired flow point for any action is somewhere below where the anxiety level is sufficient to unbalance your mind, to where the brain begins to make bad decisions due to confusion.

Rhoality Life Flow

Life Flow Potential

The sum total of your physical and mental capabilities at any time is called the life flow potential. Finding it takes trial and error, but rising anxiety in the consciousness when contemplating the end event that fulfills the action is a starting point for recognition. But, like the old saying tells us, good judgment comes from experience and experience comes from bad judgment. So, some of us will go for the highest anxiety decision and get whacked, then adjust downward. Better to go for the more cautious, lower route of lower expectations by staying just below it and let it rise over time.

Our life-flow potential should be increasingly upward slowly as we gain knowledge and experience in youth, then stay more or less level as our physical powers diminish. If indeed we can keep our body healthy, the increase in our mental abilities could keep the overall curve on

Rhoality Guide to Wellness

a positive upslope until the designed age limit prevails.

Rhoality Life Flow

Life Event Cycle

Life is ups and downs, win or lose, arrive on top, or fail. No way around that. What we need to do is to set up a flow in life where each peak and valley is higher than the previous one. Hard to do if we hit a spate of good fortune that spikes the chart. Generally, that has to come back down in our normal daily existence, which leaves us with an uneasy feeling about everything else. Winning a lottery that equals a week's pay is thrilling and pumps us up for a while, but it's not life-changing in a good sense. Mostly the change is in your attitude about what is a wise way to handle the sacrificing of instant gratification in order to build your nest egg for the future. You will always have the easy money desire in the back of your mind.

Life is a constant cycle of 'Thank you!' and 'I'm sorry!'

Tools to manage the flow:
- Self-centered as in self-forgiving.

Rhoality Guide to Wellness

- Good emotion control.
- Intellectual curiosity.
- Mind open to belief in the unprovable.
- Need to know more, sense more.
- Need for redefining self-worth higher.
- Wellness path, painfree days.
- Satisfaction with simple pleasures.
- Keen sense of dedication to fairness.

Flow Chart Use

Having a chart that represents our goals in life will help us face whatever comes. We turn negative forces that resist us to positive flow for us by an attitude of *I can* instead of *I can't*. To really believe it, you can't create a goal that would bring overwhelming doubt about its outcome. Better to go in for second place finish while still striving for first.

The feeling that things seem to be getting worse for you is good because it makes you want to think about changes for the better. This is where the yin and yang come in, where you should

Rhoality Life Flow

accept the negative instead of feeling down about it. Ancients believed that suffering was a good part of life because it pulled one down to the balance in the middle. Still, lots of people want to conclude that the negative thing isn't normal but helps keep us from getting pompous or self-assured. I think living a fully assured life is possible if only as a worthwhile goal.

The right attitude is <u>I can</u>.

The cycle that includes the wave valley is a necessary function of life. These things happen. But it's not the same as negative thoughts. They do indeed seem related and often are, but they are the power that pushes the bottom of the valley even deeper. We can't defend against all negative stimuli. Some are necessary, but a quick Entrex to return to the Rhoality state dampens the downward force.

The less time you spend in negative thoughts trying to solve mostly unsolvable attitudes of other people, the more time you have to improve your own attitude.

Rhoality Guide to Wellness

Bad things happen. But you can set the stage for their effect to be dampened by lowering your vulnerabilities to anxiety-causing events by living a risk-limiting life. Debt, risky behavior, lack of attention to family, society, or health, not tidying up loose ends when things go wrong – all can come back with a vengeance. Focus on education while still young, building a network of lifelong acquaintances, developing an attitude of being part of something bigger than yourself, limiting quick self-gratification, taking pleasure in the beauty of nature, laughter, caring for your lifelong companion, and building a support system for your family that will out-live you.

The ultimate life direction can be obtained by following the Rhoality life process of dealing with life's bumps with a calm, serene confident approach, instead of forcing actions and events. It's hard to not be forceful and just let it go but the most productive way is to lose the expressive ego.

Rhoality Life Flow

You will want to set up a process to structure a Rho line, a life path that creates a quiet faith in the future regardless of events. They don't always occur as we would like but taken overall, each one is a step toward life's end event.

For the chosen life structure and goals, it is critical that the chosen future is full of high probability visions. Normal wishful thinking would have us end up either wealthy, famous, popular, admired, adored, worshiped, powerful, or influential, among lesser goals. No one actively strives to do all these at once. We usually settle for one at a time as circumstances allow. The trick is to take these in small steps, building our base for further rungs on the ladder.

As time goes by, recent events should see the positive peaks higher and the valleys not so deep.

Surfer

Rhoality Guide to Wellness

You should try to design your flow to move like a surfer. You get positioned right, then ride the wave to the shore. You don't try to over-manage the process. That would only unbalance yourself.

The top of the wave is not the place to be. You have to find the sweet spot on your life's wave and ride it, not trying to hurry past it. Let the wave push you along. Life has a predetermined flow for you at birth. Your life possibilities open up into a cornucopia of good end events. So be sure to stay within the boundaries of highest probability vs lowest probability curves, somewhere near the middle.

For more details, refer to Appendix A.

Gaining Gratitude

It's easy enough to see how we can gain gratitude from others. That leads to much of this calm confidence we need as well as making future help from others an ingredient in the

Rhoality Life Flow

mortar that holds the blocks of our structure together. Knowing your base is firm allows you to keep your eyes upward. It also causes your positive vibes to excite others in your favor. Start with the simple flows to boost faith, confidence, and belief. Learn to recognize emotional overload in others and try to relieve it.

Overcoming Bad Judgment

The worst combination is good intentions and poor judgment. The more you try to overcome the judgment mistakes with lots of good work the worse it gets. Especially if you can't think fast on your feet.

A life flow ceiling is the anxiety point above which a decision overly decoheres and confuses the mind. A Rho line is a timeline over a life span that denotes the maximum anxiety for end events above which the Rho state has difficulty controlling.

Rhoality Guide to Wellness

Where does balance fit into social mores? One evil act brands you as evil even if you do many good things. A selfish act can be balanced by doing an equally good deed.

Managing Expectations

Rules for managing Rho flow analysis:
• Give yourself time.
• Adapt to changing expectations.
• Don't judge yourself harshly.
• Communicate - articulate the task.
• Prepare for problems.
• Predict other people's expectations.

First-place finishes are fun but come at a price. If you'd come in second, your next goal would be just one step up, predefined, and much more within your envisioning. First-place brings a false sense of security and tempts you to settle down into an easy but pressure-packed set of expectations for the next step. If you had planned your effort to have a second place but that turns out to be a first-place win, although

Rhoality Life Flow

exciting and highly motivating, the realization that you really didn't expect it should be enough to keep the lid on your expectations even through the rosy glow of success. As Kipling said, triumph and disaster are both imposters, so a pursuit of a first-place win could unbalance your mind. The brain may opt out if it decides that it is not in your nature. The moral of that story is to never leave your confidence zone.

So, follow your chart to be the best you can be. It would be great if we could be the best in the world but it's OK If not. Don't set the bar for the highest leap at the start. Set it to where you know you can make it without undue anxiety. You will eventually make it. Then let your confidence determine when to stop competing and achieve contentment.

To develop a sense of self-worth, don't overshoot the end events. Lots of tiny successes do the trick.

The Rho line at retirement time is when control plummets, influence is down, resources fade,

Rhoality Guide to Wellness

contacts grow stale, favors among colleagues are fewer, knowledge is older, physical attractiveness fades, energy levels drop. It is time to create a mini habitat, the best one being a Rho villa (see Appendix C). It could take years to build and fine-tune it, so start early in life.

Live well. That means maintaining a healthy body and mind leading to a stress-free life. But there are downsides to be wary of and control:

- A false sense of security since may not be as aware of current events.
- Have to ramp up energy when survival stimulus arrives.
- Can be seen as too laid back and viewed as noncompetitive.
- Less likely to seek fun experiences with others.
- Find it hard to want to take action like should be done.
- No determination to not defer to others when necessary.
- Having an open mind often prevents us from being quick-minded. We have to consider

Rhoality Life Flow

many possibilities before answering. When we don't, we sound odd.

The upside can override the downside by:
- Accomplishment of end events.
- Obvious good fortune.
- Make fewer enemies.
- Better health.
- Less wasted time.

Envy and jealousy can be destabilizers, but they also can be motivators that focus the mind. The same if they are allowed to create anger. It can go either way. Good or bad.

Envying someone defines better what you really want. It can be the first step in creating a desire for the beginning of envisioning.

Managing expectations with highs and lows emotionally is the same. Losing the game means that your mind has cleared a space for something better. But when you win at everything, you could have a hard time handling defeat when it comes.

Rhoality Guide to Wellness

Anticipate bumps, then shoot them down. Promise less than you can deliver.

Humble Majesty

We think of someone royal as being majestic because they are allowed the final say-so over everyone else and use it in their daily decision-making. We will define majesty as the feeling that we have found the handle on the door to the path to the secret of life.

No one chastises the king for acting majestic.

The Rhoality definition of majesty: *I made the decision. I don't know if it was right for everyone, but it was my decision to make. I take responsibility for the results. I did my best so I don't feel guilty and will not take remedial action or change my mind just to suit you.*

Rhoality Life Flow

That's my majesty talking. Your personal feeling about your use of majesty should rise in life along the life flow line.

When you realize that you control your future through Rhoality, the first thing you feel is that slight sense of majesty that you belong to a unique group of people who hold a special place. When others sense it in you, you feel it and your belief becomes absolute. Guard it carefully from your other inner self.

Majesty in Rhoality comes with that quiet confidence in the future. It says that you have the knowledge and are living the path that you have established, you are confident that you are where you belong and can help others to come up to where you are. It has many of the same attributes as self-realization.

Humility is maintaining that sense of majesty while not allowing it to be diluted by allowing something someone said or did to make you think that they should make your decision for you, without your having a sense of superiority.

Rhoality Guide to Wellness

There should be nothing fake about majesty. It should show itself only when humility has set the stage. An open mind is an admission that you have doubt that you know everything. It is the precursor of intellectual curiosity.

But what if I really desire to be rich and powerful. Possible, but remember, greed for power corrupts and unbalances us. A small subset of people with a harsh genetic makeup in survival programming, feelings of greed, and non-empathy and sacrifice of the body, seem to have it all. The price they pay is often hidden and far too high to abandon all the simple pleasures of life for it.

Rhomers

People who have discovered that Rhoality works for them are called Rhomers. They quickly develop a deeply felt but rarely shown majestic attitude. Self-centered, but not selfish, not condescending, not overbearing.

Rhoality Life Flow

Rhomers believe that they have found a path to the best life possible simply because they are open-minded enough to develop the idea. They live so as to not create and to even lessen anxiety for everyone they come in contact with. They hold up their end of the social contract and try to leave others, especially those who have shared their world, better off for having cared for them. Neither they nor those who have benefitted from the mutual guardianship will ever know what powers were unleashed by the other one's goodwill near the end of life. The satisfaction for both is immense.

For a Rhomer, majesty is confidence that this basic secret of the universe was designed for them, and maybe somewhere out there is a creator who must have some sort of satisfaction that their design for humans was being used and appreciated.

How do Rhomers get these benefits without envisioning? By relaxing, letting it take care of you. When you push it, like asking for an unreasonable raise at work, you force it to re-determine paths that it has already found for

Rhoality Guide to Wellness

you. That predetermined path would move you along the bottom of your flow line. When you try to punch through it by envisioning a shortcut, which is usually based on impatience or greed, it gets tricky on how it turns out and even trickier to get a new project on the line. It can be done, but why would you?

Rhomers don't seem vulnerable since they don't project anxiety.

Self-love

Some people spend their life trying to build esteem in the world's eyes. Achievement is one thing that works, but the feeling that you have to charm the opposite sex for them to esteem you is a losing proposition from the start. But you find you're good at it, so it continues and the pleasure of the esteem allows it to slide into addiction. You need to deal with this type of negative thinking as quickly as possible before it has you making self-defeating decisions that

Rhoality Life Flow

keep you from getting back to life in a positive mode.

The response to an emerging guilty feeling is self-forgiveness, which eventually leads to self-acceptance, the door to self-love.

Selfless or Unconditional Love

Selfless love can be damaging like extreme pain. It is better to be interconnected through loving others as part of yourself. The mind has to temper it or it may become destructive to any flow because we cannot control it. Maybe it heals somehow but more likely it produces anxiety in the shadows in another person.

Over time, communing with someone in short intervals can result in near-perfect entrainment. This is somewhat negated by the feeling of one person that the other isn't as dedicated to it.

Rhoality Guide to Wellness

Flow to Health

Flow is where health begins. Go from one positive thought to another and make the breaks short and not impactful in any way. Our life needs to flow on its own coherent course. It will lead to good events if we don't try to leap ahead of the flow.

Living calmly can be seen as a weakness by those who don't understand us. A Romer must present a firm and consistent front that looks solid in resources and is almost unassailable from the outside. For Rhomers, having a feeling of belonging to a like-minded group goes a long way toward that.

Appendix A

Notes

Rhoality Guide to Wellness

Peak Management

The surfer will ride the front side of a peak but never allow it to catch up. Success depends on staying ahead of the top in order to be gone when the peak reaches there. We can't ride a single wave far. For example, if we're about to receive an award, we use the pre-event surge in feeling to get the next event going. By the time the peak that is due to the award is present, we're using its power impulse for the next one.

The wave determines the push. You can't speed it up or make it more powerful, just take what it gives you, which is all right. It's there for you. Remember, you are the end product of millions of years of evolution.

If the flow line could use the peak as the start of a new upward move, lots of spikes would be good. But the shadows that accompany a big change, even an upward one, bring with them a whole new set of worries, doubts, and fears. The spike quickly sees a downside as the consequences of dealing with the big success set

Appendix A Notes

in. Even a promotion brings uncertainty, loss of relationships, and fear of unknown tensions, all by simply pulling us out of the Rho state we have used for comfort. As the aftereffects of wealth and power threaten to keep us awake at night, it gets harder to keep the quiet faith in ourselves. We are pushed by others and our own knowledge of our poor preparation for the anxieties of being in the fishbowl that a higher level on the socio-economic pyramid brings.

Each point on your flow line requires a certain amount of wealth (assets) to keep money from becoming a chronic worry. Above that, having much more than that amount rarely leads to a net positive ending.

Keep in mind that the objective is to live a full, healthy life, however long that turns out to be. Peaks, those anxiety producing events like winning, thrills, attainment, wealth, bursts of emotion highs, hubris, etc, are highly sought after, but all are expensive to get in terms of attaining our goal. Better to be like the surfer, near the peak but never letting it catch you. *How sweet it is* applies to every morning you

Rhoality Guide to Wellness

wake up in old age and feel good, knowing your efforts have gotten you there.

Appendix A Notes

Predicting Events

Predicting is how we try to make life easier for ourselves by making the right decisions. We want to respond correctly to what we think people's reaction to what we say and do will be. We base our actions on our experiences – past events that are stored in our memory. We pull them out and along with the emotions attached to them, use as much of this data as we can find to make a decision. Our conscious mind can put these to use but can focus on only one at a time and accumulate and stir everything together to get an overall feeling about the situation and where it will take us. As in our need to focus on each stimulus, our conscious mind is limited by reality.

We spend much of our time predicting. If you want to decide on whether to take an umbrella with you, you look at the sky and remember what you have heard about rain this week, then predict what your next action should be from these few data points. As usual, it turns out to be hit or miss. If you knew more about the humidity and where else it was raining, wind direction around you and the temperature of the air in several places, you could make a more accurate prediction. The weather station does know these things and uses its computer to analyze it all for their predictions, which are pretty good but obviously far from perfect. Finally, if you had knowledge of every drop of moisture floating in the air, the temperature and direction of all levels of wind, plus the result of situations in the past very much like these that resulted in rain, you could get near total accuracy.

However, it would take a quantum computer to be able to constantly analyze such a vast amount of data and do its prediction. Fortunately, the Rho Matrix in the brain is a quantum computer and is constantly using data from the Rho Field (space between atoms in the brain) and analyzing it along with the latest current stimuli in order to determine the many paths that we could take.

The Rho Matrix calculates the wave function for each event for each possible path with a

Appendix A Notes

different set of information for each decision in an event. It then puts them together to get the final probabilities sent to the brain in the cloud. But even though the Rho Matrix gives us a great number of choices, our consciousness can deal with only one at a time and even task-sharing does not allow us to be able to use much of what is available. That is why envisioning is so important. It creates the list of what is most important to us.

Even by itself, using this vast amount of information would allow an extremely high predictability of each event path. But the quantum nature of the brain allows an even higher level. In quantum physics, time marches to its own drummer. The past, present, and future are essentially all one, and we sense time as only a way of determining the sequence of events. The Rho Matrix has the ability to play out the possible event path beyond the current time to see how things turn out.

Rhoality Guide to Wellness

Envisioning

Daydreaming is a form of envisioning. It simultaneously calms our minds and more clearly defines what event direction would give us what we desire. It is stress-free thought that allows us to become coherent.

When a Rho vision is created under the Rho process, that is, starting with a serene, balanced mind, deep thoughts on just what the end event should look like, careful concern of the consequences of getting what we want over the wishes of others, managing bad things that happen along the way (bumps), thought over whether the end event will accomplish what we really want to happen, ensuring that overriding our life flow line doesn't push our anxiety level beyond our brain's coherency level, some tiny nagging doubts could start about whether we truly believe it will happen.

Responding to a stimulus like sudden dark clouds in the sky is in its highest form a survival response. At a lower level, getting pelted by

Appendix A Notes

hail, though more probable than getting swept away by a tornado, still sends the body into survival mode. We confront these actions countless times in a normal day and generally find it easy to return to a more clam, relaxed state. Our only recourse is to avoid what the forces of nature outside our control have in store for us.

Beyond survival, the hierarchy of needs for people moves rapidly into more mundane daily life. We can daydream, be attracted to others, seek esteem in our groups, and generally pursue the various pleasure-based events of life in reality. This is where Rhoality really comes into its own. Above and beyond the health motivations of positive thinking, Entrex, and brain self-healing, our brains can enhance our future even more since every event that requires a decision on our part has an EWF associated with it.

Rhoality Guide to Wellness

Health

In theory, people who get a placebo should expect the same results as those who get real medicine. Unfortunately, most trial participants know that there is a possibility that they have received a placebo, which adds doubt to the process. For a placebo to work, the brain must be convinced that help is on the way. Any doubt can undo a successful result.

Not knowing whether you received one skews all placebo-based trials. Some of the placebo receivers would believe they got the medicine and would be healed similar to a non-placebo controlled group.

Appendix A Notes

The Healing Power of Touch

Healing by the power of the human touch is underused by medical science. Simple things like handshakes and hugs bring us pleasant feelings that help calm us.

Two magnets with overlapping fields will affect each other. As their fields vibrate, their frequencies naturally try to entrain, that is, become more like each other. One slows down while the other one speeds up. The closer the magnets are, the more powerful the effect.

People are meant to be together. Even loners feel different when someone non-negative is nearby. Like much of the quantum world, quantum, entrainment comes through magnetic fields and more so through humans touching. Two bodies in resonance are vibrating in an octave relationship and entrainment is automatic. Perfect resonance is rare. When found, it should be cherished and guarded.

People are magnets and subtly feel entrainment, the mutual preening of people's

Rhoality Guide to Wellness

body aura, when close to someone else. When one who has constant static in their brain, that is, lots of decoherence, comes within the magnetic aura of someone who is in the calm Rho state; that is, a balanced and coherent aura, they both can feel it consciously. One feels a calming effect while the other feels a tiny burst of energy.

Touching releases endorphins – stress and pain-fighting hormones. In fact, it works better on chronic illnesses than acute ones. Repeated touching increases the entrainment. Touching is powerful, and over time, entrainment works so well that they both seem to be able to read each other's mind.

Touch is the surest path to healing the brain. Moving within another person's aura can come about by simple nearness, allowing the bodies' magnetic fields to overlap, and hopefully entrain. Other factors, like similar wave functions and brain entanglement through DNA, embellish the force and guide entrainment. But

Appendix A Notes

the power of intimate touch is the ultimate balancing process.

Unfortunately, modern social mores define all touch between strangers to be a result of attraction. And, with separation for health reasons now more important than inclusion for bonding becoming the standard, finding others with like auras by touch is much more restrictive. Indeed, keeping focused on the goal is not always possible. When prurient Interest rises, all else fades. Even romantic sparks can push our interest far from the original goal, although these feelings of belonging with someone can be the catalyst for a deep friendship.

Appendix B
Topics for Discussion

Appendix B Topics

Healing Touch

Most of my experimenting with touch entrainment came when interpersonal touching was deemed an acceptable way to indicate approval and desire for a closer relationship, especially between friends and others in our social groups. It was OK and even expected. Gentlemen would guide their lady through doorways and the best of friends could stroll hand in hand.

Later trials were generally dropped early as others signed onto the mantra that touch without permission had evil or selfish intent behind it. Indeed, even between two people with matching auras, it's not easy to keep it all down to earth. The more needy someone is for intimacy, the less likely it is that the other person will be comfortable for long.

So, touchy procedures with strangers is out. The less powerful process of nearness and analysis of events and experienced feeling is the far better path.

Rhoality Guide to Wellness

The Healer

A healer is someone whose impact on another's aura causes an increase in the balance, coherence, understanding, or desire to be a better person. Impacts include inner response to touch, damping of anxiety, increase in majesty, or a deepening belief in one's own capability to belong to a select group.

Some people are natural healers without knowledge of it. They heal by instinct and the feeling of entrained auras. They are not always virtuous but the lack of unbalancing emotional trauma from having hurt another person, physical or mentally, paves the way for healing actions as a daily natural response to others.

Can anyone be healed? The best shot is between two people whose auras match. The frequency of our own fields resonates with overlapping similar ones. The body's field can be measured as a bubble maybe 10 feet across but can possibly affect someone far away at a lower

Appendix B Topics

sensitivity level. We should ask ourselves how many pulls toward a stranger in life have we mistaken for something else.

When we become a healer, we share responsibility for their happiness and, to some extent, for their survival.

Rhoality Guide to Wellness

Resisting Mind Control

The future of the world passed one of the most important milestones in history when artificial intelligence was developed. Little did they know how it would be turned into a master of the human mind. In the hands of fanatical power-hungry elites, control of our own futures has been passed to those who can manipulate knowledge, the ultimate power. As we become more dependent on electronic gadgets to take over our daily burdens, we slowly cede the right to a private life to them.

Now deep into the twenty-first century, we can read thoughts, create designer people, manage the truth (or untruth) of the history of not only nations and sacred institutions but also of everyone's personal life. To a prospective friend or employer, whatever your internet file says about you is gospel, even if you weren't the author or even cognizant that anything at all was assigned to you as being your performed actions or thoughts.

Appendix B Topics

Alas, predicting how this will turn out even in our lifetimes isn't all that hard. A few at the top of the socio-economic pyramid now are aware and pressing development of these tools of tomorrow, today. They own the research institutions that will own the power that will own us. The pyramid will turn into a cork floating on a vast sea of helpless workers, subdued by a mind control school that prepares us at an early age to take what they give us and be happy. If we want out, we will be like the unfortunate borrowers in the control of the loan sharks who ensure that they owe more tomorrow than now. Without a sympathetic government to hold this back, they will be caught in a whirlwind of reaction to others' whims, burdened by a harsh package of lies and an even harsher load of debt.

How do we resist? Only those who can foresee the methods that will be used to get on top of us will have a shot at it.

When they capture your brain waves, their machines will turn it all into words. You most likely won't even know. Only through

Rhoality Guide to Wellness

preparation to block your own mind can it be resisted. Locking into the Rho State closes off the reality access to the conscious mind from the outside.

Appendix B Topics

Justifying our Self-interest

Most of the things we want in life will also be sought by other people. We like to think of ourselves as generous and fair to everyone, but as we look deeper into the meaning of those terms, we see that they are relative to only those in our nearby society. We handle that inequity by a series of rationalizations that seem to justify our place in the socio-economic pyramid that would stretch to include all of humanity. But even if it were possible to provide an equal sharing of the world's resources, the practical pitfalls quickly push us back into believing that it is best for all involved for us to work within the laws and mores of our locality, however you would define that. In our society, the process of wealth distribution is based on practicality. It includes:

- There not being enough to go around, so some will by default have more than their share.
- Best choices should perhaps go to the best people. Some deserve more than others if

Rhoality Guide to Wellness

they contribute more (harder workers, smarter, have more creativity, etc).

- There is a need to have inherited wealth so we aren't constantly fighting over it.
- Everyone should be free to decide who they share their wealth with.
- We can't change much anyway. Birth parents have already decided most things for us: physical and mental abilities; health at birth and early years; diet; attitudes; attractiveness, common sense, maybe; wealth to enable us to get tools to compete in life. Could also add in here luck, first come first served, etc.

The one other thing that further supports this generous self-interest is our own brain. As it cranks us through our reality, it first and last tries to maintain its own life support, our own body. If that is threatened, it has an automatic gear change to ensure survival, regardless. That includes self-preservation, safety of others that we consider necessary (family, friends), then lesser ones (acquaintances, those with similar

Appendix B Topics

morality, most like us in thought and deed, organizations we support, esoteric things like culture, history, even nature).

When threats to any of these things put us into what is surely survival mode at some level, we would like to quickly resolve the issue and return to a more enjoyable state of mind and body. Not easy when our day is full of threats of one kind or another. Regardless of our wealth or status, someone is working to push us down the pyramid. In a normal day, there is no calm, serene reality mental state that allows us to handle it all without stress, even if temporarily. This means that in our usual mini-panic existence, our poor addled brain is just as likely to do us harm as be an aid. It certainly is not likely to provide us with the right decisions to get us out of the problems.

All this is to say that life is justifiably competitive. It is good to use the neglected (or forgotten) quantum feature inside our brain to help us along.

Rhoality Guide to Wellness

If you allow your temptations to cloud your mind, its no wonder that you stray from your chosen path when they arise.

Appendix C
Triverity

The Very Man is out of print, so the section on Triverity, the three pillars of Rhoality, is reprinted here in its entirety.

Rhoality Guide to Wellness

Authors Note

When the number of unexplained fortunate coincidences, those that over our lifetime have saved us from the folly of bad judgment and rash decisions, becomes so large that they are impossible to ignore, we have to start believing in the possibility that our guardian angels just might be real. Not easy when you are a reasonably scientifically minded cause-and-effect believer.

The one huge barrier to belief that I couldn't quite get over was the possibility of self-delusion. So, the problem became how to prove that all the largess emanating from a creator of life could be scientifically possible without leaning on rationalization as smoking-gun proof. Research led me to write *Power of the Quantum Mind,* how the quantum mind works. It is a straightforward summary of brain science with a toe dipped into metascience, necessary since we can

Appendix C Triverity

peer directly into the brain but not into the mind.

Amazingly, the process I was seeking slowly emerged, then coalesced into a new theory of how people have been able to be, as we like to say, favored by the gods. I call this theory Triverity for the three pillars it rests upon: quantum science, the brain-cosmos connection, and personal anecdotes of how good fortune has transcended any possibility of random chance. My hope is that someone reading this will be inspired or at least curious enough to find out whether it works for them also.

Rhoality Guide to Wellness

Introduction

The brain has long been recognized as a quantum object. It teems with quantum behavior inside its atoms and is the main source of information for us about the physical world that exists, mostly through photons, objects we call light. Science tells us that every particle in the universe has a wave nature so must be collapsed by an observer before it can exist in our reality. This quantum world has the inconvenient characteristic of being impossible to prove with a smoking gun proof. So, better to sidestep the how and why and just discover how to use it to make things work right for ourselves.

But once we accept the merging of science and the metascience we call quantum physics, we can move forward into creating reasonably determined science-based models that can explain the anecdotal events that we have often refused to believe could possibly exist. One of these is that the brain can

Appendix C Triverity

connect to the amazing amount of energy that makes up most of our brain space and contains an unbelievable amount of information soaked up over the past millennia. Indeed, explaining the possibility of how it works should open the door to more and stronger belief, which is key to its success in the first place. Add to that the quantum principle that nothing exists until observed by consciousness and you get the rule that life is indeed a self-fulfilling prophecy. Or, as they say, as the twig is bent the tree is inclined, meaning that if you control the little stuff, you can create the big ones.

Triverity describes the three pillars of truth that outline the workings of the quantum mind that lead to Rhoality, which includes the science of quantum event collapse. These events create our reality and are based on the metascience of the quantum state of the mind, the Rho state. It reveals how those who can control it are able to access the brain energy and data and manipulate them via the event collapses to their own benefit. It also

Rhoality Guide to Wellness

explains Entrex, the simple and straightforward act of consciousness that provides entry into the Rho state for those who believe it will work.

Triverity Pillars

- The Event Wave Function (EWF)
- Rho State Living
- Entrex

The Event Wave Function

Triverity Pillar 1

Rhoality Guide to Wellness

Rhoality vs Reality

Reality is the brain's take on what is in its environment. Rhoality is the full experience of the quantum connection to reality. Reality is presented to us by images in the mind that let us live through time in a motion picture. Rhoality is hidden in the space inside and between the atoms in the brain (Rho space) and must have its results turned into reality before we can comprehend its effects and allow the conscious mind to create what we think of as awareness.

Our reality isn't made aware of what is happening inside the quantum mind area. The brain is aware of many things that are not brought into focus long enough to register in our memory as a true awareness, such as fleeting images or sensory stimuli. If one's mind is busy thinking of something else, the unaware things won't register even as brainwave fluctuations. Thus, any quantum action in the brain is of such short duration

Appendix C Triverity

that it doesn't register or disturb the neuron voltage output commonly probed in an EEG.

Brain make-up

The physical brain consists of clusters of what we think of as matter arranged into atoms with a nucleus and a number of electrons somewhere nearby. Think of them as being a cloud of probabilities we can't see into, so we don't know for sure where in this cloud the electrons are. It remains this way until something like our conscious mind actually observes it, when it does what in physics is called a quantum collapse. The action of the observer causes the selection of one location for the electron. If observed in a different manner, the result is different. This indicates that the mind really does control the future of matter and is the basis for the possibility that we can train our minds to have an impact on our own future.

Also inside the brain is lots of space, actually over 99.999% of the volume. Not empty space, though, it's full of energy that is packed with information that has been

Rhoality Guide to Wellness

absorbed by the energy field and is accessible to other quantum features in the brain. This data is a complete record of events that have taken place involving human decision making and what the results were.

The Rho quantum state

One feature of the brain is the quantum computing power that resides inside cells and a similar power within the brain energy field. Classical psychology defines the brain states that go from the lowest brain wave frequency (Delta) during sleep to the highest (Gamma) during high anxiety. The quantum brain state (Rho) is physically less definable and centers around the transition from the middle reality mind state Alpha (daydreams) to Theta (subconscious). This is where our conscious and subconscious minds meet. This state handles the quantum connection to the brain space energy field (the Rho field) and handshakes with the brain through its magnetic field and quantum entanglement.

Appendix C Triverity

This makes the Rho field data accessible to our conscious mind.

Mental states and stimuli

The mental states of reality are defined by frequency ranges that can be measured by an EEG wave trace. The Rho state, which overlies perhaps all the central reality states, works at an extremely fast rate so does not visibly affect the brainwaves in any measurable manner. The quantum fluctuations are small and independent of the emotional context that drives our reality wave changes. The Rho mind has to handle not only quantum functions such as cloud event collapse but also must keep the information contained in the Rho field up to date. This is the data set area that aids the mind in its decisions when making further collapses. If you stare at an unchanging scene like a blank wall, there is no discernible change in reality then, but the photons coming to your eyes still must all be collapsed constantly, movement or not. To slow it all down you would have to be able to shut out all of the stimuli that drive reality, but you can't because internal body actions are the biggest part of it. Organs are still working, blood is still flowing, magnetic fields still fluctuating. Then add to all that motion the stimuli from normally non-aware external sources, like gamma rays, quantum entanglements, and external magnetic fields. These sources likely contribute a large amount of unseen, undetected stimuli so that event collapsing barely lessens even without detected changes.

Creativity and imagination

Creativity is a mind feature that results from another feature called imagination. It pulls data from our memory and the subconscious mind and receives it from the software-like process in the Rho space called the Rho Matrix. This process gives us ideas that have never been introduced to the brain before but are stored in the Rho field because they likely happened once upon a time to us or some other consciousness. The Rho Matrix

Appendix C Triverity

has been described as a virtual reality system that the mind has been plugged into.

Event Wave Function EWF

The nature of quantum collapse has been known to science for almost a hundred years. Einstein called parts of quantum science spooky action at a distance. Although widely acknowledged as true physics, it really is metaphysics, so how it works has been ignored in favor of learning how to use it. Early experiments to at least corral it in resulted in even more magic, such as defining just what collapses, which actually is the wave function, another physics term. It has to do with the wave nature of all particles and their characteristic probabilities. But the nature of experiments is such that they have results that can't be pinned down to a single property, like spin or location. They are described in terms of the upper-level physics (that enables reality) that rests atop the quantum physics (that enables Rhoality). This creates a strange being called the event wave function (EWF) to handle the collapse of the experiment results from a cloud of possibilities to a single result. Niels Bohr, an early pioneer in the quantum nature of atoms, described the EWFs as *hovering* around the experiment, then collapsing to a result upon being observed.

It gets stranger. Where do these EWFs come from? Event Collapse Theory (James Circe, Power of the Quantum Mind) describes them as originating in the conscious mind whenever a future event or situation is envisioned. The Rho Matrix maintains it and updates the progress of the EWF until the event occurs, the originator forgets it or reality changes enough to make it impossible.

Envisioning

Envisioning is giving substance to an imagined event. The EWF created at the start contains an impossibly large number of possibilities to make any sense, and the farther away it is in time, the harder that task is. As time passes,

Appendix C Triverity

it all becomes clearer to our mind as the possibilities become fewer.

But, hold on. This cloud of possibilities called an event is also collapsed by an observation and that means that the observer can help determine the nature of the collapse, if we can envision it in a clear enough fashion that the Rho Matrix can determine the gillions (pick a big number) of events that have to occur along the way. This is called the event path and the final goal is called the end event.

State table

A reasonable form for describing this mechanism to the software-minded observer is what is termed a state-stimulus table. This is a decision table that predetermines the action that must be taken for a goal to be reached, based on what the current state is. Each state has a finite number of possible ways it can be moved from its current state toward the goal. When one of these stimuli occurs, the Matrix looks into its own internal state table to find these possibilities and presents it to the conscious mind in a list (cloud) of actions, listed in probability order, for the conscious mind to select from.

The mind analyzes each one along with the emotions it has stored in memory to determine which possibility will get it to the end event with the least harm to its internal morality or even inconvenience limit. The decision is shared with the Matrix, the event is collapsed and the state tables are updated by the Rho Matrix to be used for the next event.

Other people affected

Envisioning occurs where the consciousness meets the subconsciousness. Science tells us that Imagination originates in the reality mind states that are analogous to the Rho state. If the brain is clear on what the vision is and has no confusion or conflict in the desired result, after creating the EWF for the desired event it then passes control to the Rho Matrix to maintain it. Since it is quantum entangled

Appendix C Triverity

with the Rho field, it knows where to read the state tables of other consciousnesses and where to access all their event wave functions in order to fill out and update its own table with that new data.

Are there too many brains with too many possible paths to have to handle here? Not really, if you consider that the only ones that are managed constantly by any brain Matrix are the ones created in the Rho state of a balanced brain because only they are required to access quantum paths and events in order to manage the tables to the end event. Others are managed at a physical level, if managed at all.

It is possible that the EWF management takes place only while the mind is in the Rho state, and certainly for the ones that originate there. That would explain why influencing future events works so well for Rhomers (since they have a natural Rho state access and live mainly in Rhoality) and why they are required to return to the Rho state so often to get the best results.

Rho State Living
Triverity Pillar 2

The basics of Rho State Living begins with Circe's original description of the Rho state and how it was first put into play by people who had no certain knowledge of what had been given to them when they would pause and suddenly realize that someone, or something, was protecting them and even allowing them to seek good things in the future just by wishing it to be true. In retrospect, coming to the necessary level of belief in a guardian angel of sorts had to have taken a long time and a large number of coincidences that finally collected into a critical mass that simply wouldn't allow any doubt.

Circe: To access the powers of the cosmos connection, we need take our minds no

Appendix C Triverity

deeper than the area between the Alpha and Theta states, which we'll term the Rho state. This is the quantum state of the brain and can access the information in the Rho space.

Rhomers

People who have a well-developed set of subconscious response reactions can access the power of quantum event collapses to set the tone for future events. These folks are known as Rhomers. From *Power of the Quantum Mind*:

Becoming a new Rhomer.

This state can in fact be maintained in daily living under certain conditions of balance between the brain and body. This balance results from a lack of anxiety creation and is achieved by following a conscious practice of downplaying the importance of the small stuff (and, as they say, it's all small stuff). Those who have been successful at reprogramming their subconsciousness to erase the negative

Rhoality Guide to Wellness

impulses can settle into this Rho state by exercising Theta state thoughts as responses to anxiety level events before they allow the consciousness to retrieve them from deep subconscious image storage. The watchword phrase is "It doesn't matter!" no matter how traumatic the event is. When the conscious mind accepts that as truth, there is no anxiety arising from the mind demons. The brain quickly slips back into Rho state, the subconscious is subdued and placated, and the resulting mind-cosmos resonance allows for the event collapse to be positive. Rho State Theory is looking inward to be able to control the cosmos with the end goal of satisfaction in knowing that control of the future is in the right hands.

Being a natural Rhomer.

A similar path to a Rho state life is available to people who have in fact never had subconscious survival programming. This could come from a childhood lack of anxiety, the great and ruthless teacher. This may be

Appendix C Triverity

for youth who live a life of protected luxury, but most likely belongs to those who have been well taken care of but never parented harshly enough to be given reason for acquiring anxiety programming over survival state feelings. They arrive at conscious programming feeling that they aren't part of the accepted level of any society and don't expect to be able to control their part in one by any way other than being submissive, hidden, and generally living in their own fantasy world where they won't come in contact with conflict, competition or having to prove anything to anyone. Just a couple of ingrained survival feelings is sufficient to allow their conscious mind to slip into a perpetual Rho fantasy state for any event.

As data from anecdotal evidence, given by those who had realized that there must have been science behind the metascience of the Rho state, started being compiled, a search for fellow travelers turned up some basic entries that have been put forth that are

Rhoality Guide to Wellness

indicative of similar minds. Few if any had more than just a few of them.

They are possible Rhomers if they:

- Feel like they have a guardian angel.
- Are curious about quantum science and the body.
- Are curious about how the brain works.
- Want to understand their short attention span.
- Have read *A Walk with the Shadows* or *Power of the Quantum Mind.*
- Like the idea of being in a group like this.
- Are into a study of personalities.
- Are into meditation or other oriental disciplines like Yoga.
- Wonder why you're so excited about it.

Beliefs of Rhomers.

As Rhomers live the Rhoality life (live in cognizance of the quantum side of reality), experience and seasoning allow them to

Appendix C Triverity

develop belief in many of the offerings it proffers.

There is no set dogma, just a core list of observed characteristics:

• A superior intelligence called the creator made it all from energy.
• The creator made life and a livable Earth and evolved the human brain.
• The brain connects to the Rho Matrix (the intelligence in the Rho space of the brain) through magnetic fields and quantum entanglement.
• Event Collapse Theory and the Rho state explain Rhomer abilities.
• The mind uses sorted possibilities to select the next event.
• Voicing our intentions allows it to select to its advantage.
• Envisioning balances and tunes the brain for clarity.
• A natural mental state Rho exists for many people.

Rhoality Guide to Wellness

• A balanced brain is necessary for health and Rho envisioning.

• Obligation often works as well as an action to return to the Rho state.

• The conscious mind uses data from the Rho field to create the wave event cloud (EWF).

• The Rho Matrix has no emotion or morality associated with its data.

• It is best to avoid unnecessary medicine, especially gene-altering vaccines.

• The path back to the Rho state after survival recovery is over is through Entrex.

Characteristics of Rhomers (Circe).

Rhomers can access this power without going into a deep mental state or indeed having to follow any method. You may know one. They live their lives at times aloof from the cares of the world, never seeming to attach importance to the little nuisances that most people add to their daily lives that keep them in a state of anxiety, and always exhibit a calm assurance that they have control of their

Appendix C Triverity

future. They may be seen smiling and even laughing to themselves for no reason at all. A fantasy world, to be sure, but real to them.

Continually letting go of bad things that have happened is prerequisite to not having a chronic sense of anxiety due to worry, anger, or guilt. Also, poetry and music are aids to daydreaming as well as having people around you who seem to have a wave function similar to or at least tunable to yours.

Remember the old saying: conscience doth make cowards of us all. That's the old meaning of conscience, which is the fear of consequences, not guilt. That comes under worry more than guilt.

Having daily intimate contact with the earth, especially in the early formative years, is particularly helpful in creating a countering balance. And, when you live in a state of creativity instead of a state of stress, much coherence flows from the cosmos to your brain without even asking. Remember, we're not changing the world, we're changing how we perceive the world.

Asking the cosmos for a desired action reinforces the link between it and the mind. A body with all parts tuned to and in coherence with the cosmos clears the pipeline for help. Real intimacy in life is what you have inside, how you feel about being with yourself. Your mind has to be able to trust your subconscious or it will never find balance. The purpose of survival reprogramming is to regain that trust. A conflicted existence means random and messy results.

The pivotal action of being in the Rho fantasy state is daydreaming. It can be found without closing out the entire real world by being in a place of exceptional serenity and isolation. This can be aided by having a full plate of interests, expectations, happy thoughts, lovely people in daily contact, hope for the future, and a pain-free day. And it doesn't help if you allow bad events to loom or dwell

Appendix C Triverity

on their possibility, so take care of business before seeking entry.

Not being burdened by the anxieties of the past is key to a balanced future but living in this state is not without its costs. The absence of these behavior modifiers allows obsessions and addictions to find a shortcut to influence in responses to event stimuli. Rationalization becomes the first defense, and a plan must be put in place to balance the results.

In order to live in a Rho state, the mind must be in the right mental state. To assist the process, a program called Rho State Living (RSL) is a mental software state machine creation program that is the replacement for the meditation-deleted hard-wired ones that used to be enabled by the subconscious when the corresponding stress stimuli were received. How the Rho matrix makes its decisions is one of two possible ways. The matrix and the brain both have what we call a state machine to limit the possibly infinite number of possibilities for the event. That prescribes the possible event based on an

Rhoality Guide to Wellness

incoming stimulus and what the current state is. The cosmos has such a table available and is constantly being updated. The second way they can connect is through their quantum computing power. They have the capability to analyze a near-infinite number of options in a short time, probably fast enough to do so before it becomes a collapse.

Creating this program in the subconscious is a conscious exercise combined with meditation.

A few of the self-described emotions associated with living in the Rho state are:

- Live in one's mind, fantasy world.
- Daydreaming, lots of dream time.
- Open-minded about unknown.
- Feel disturbance in the force.
- Join minds - mind channeling.
- Display some artistic ability.
- Like physical contact with like-minded others.

Appendix C Triverity

- Swap consciousness a lot.
- Have late-stage survival programming.
- Don't embarrass much or at all.
- Tend to rush into doing things that almost will surely turn out bad.
- The feeling of having to seem to be ahead of or better than anyone you talk to or that their misfortune makes you look better to them in comparison. Strange, but it is the basis for most human interactions.
- Lack of sharing others' pain. Rhomers care just as much as others when something bad happens to someone else, they just don't allow the reaction response to overpower their minds. It's more of a deep sense of loss that displays as more of a numbness and can last a lifetime.
- Experience sadness when: see a child crying, in pain or broken and unfixable; any honest person seeing their dreams shattered; grieving for a child; man realizing he can't do anything more for his family; a preteen finding out what the world thinks of them; anyone who tries hard but gets embarrassed for not getting there.

Rhoality Guide to Wellness

• Find themselves laughing for no reason, maybe due to a large amount of Serotonin left free to act when Enteric brain is relaxed.

• Try to not focus on how one might fail, rather focus on how one can succeed.

• Realize that anger decoheres the brain and requires this deep state rewiring, so give special dispensation to unloved, unexpected, uncaring and insensitive, otherwise low self-esteem people.

• Know that worry can be dispensed by thinking *Nothing I do can except lower my self-esteem, so don't worry.*

• Smooth anger by thinking *I don't expect better because I haven't earned it.*

• Love less but understandably so since friends flee.

• Fight when have to, otherwise totally avoid confrontation.

• Can't always think fast.

• Do not take responsibility for the way they are. Subconscious programming overpowers *I am* and results *in I am not.*

Appendix C Triverity

- Relieve guilt by realizing *I really had no choice.*
- No chronic worry, anger or guilt.
- Lack of empathy due to suppression of deep emotions to the surface.
- Have always felt that a guardian angel is nearby.
- Try to be a guardian for someone else.
- No shame. *You know how I am.* Feel like am worthless to others but have deep-seated and unshakable self-worth.

Religious people often ask why the creator doesn't answer all prayers, particularly for guilt. Most people, religious or not, have chronic guilt. Forgiveness by others does not erase guilt, it just blanks out the fear of consequences. Rhomers, instead of conflicting over what is right and wrong, balance action by creating the obligation to take other actions that erase the negative loss they have handed to others. The keywords are *I'll make it up*. Guilt doesn't make sense and Rhomer action is intended to

Rhoality Guide to Wellness

be in one's self-interest, leaving questions of conscience to other mind functions.

Conscience in this sense means fear of consequences as in the old days. Fear brings worry, so consciousness must stay clear of things like fear of future events, fear *of I do I don't.* The basis of worry is the presence of presumed helplessness when and if an event occurs.

Rhoality

Rhoality embodies the experience of living with a quantum brain. It would be considered a quantum reality if it were interpretable by the mind, but its workings remain hidden to our reality. Its results are the basis for a far more comforting life than the false reality our brain normally presents to us.

Review

Define Bump – event in chosen path that is now recognized as being unacceptable.

Appendix C Triverity

Define end event – the goal that the imagination has set up as its desired situation or event. Ultimate end of and definition of event in EWF.

Define Entrainment

When two objects share their characteristics such that they both change to be more like each other.

Imagination

In the cosmos-brain boundary, the connection part of the workings of the mind allows our understanding of physics to revert to a totally reason-based cause and effect, else we would never be sure that our actions will be taken seriously after event collapse. That means that a model of the brain having a quantum computer but returning numbers we can use simply lets us envision it as a computer running classical software algorithms. We call the reality part of it the mind and the quantum part, the Rho Matrix.

Event collapse decisions are based on logical goals over a logical path and set in motion by

Rhoality Guide to Wellness

logical actions. No magic anywhere. The brain tends to the health business of the body while the Rho Matrix sets up the necessary workings to guide us to the end event. It may be true at this point to envision the connection as an entangled quantum computer that drives how our reality plays out. Thus, the state stimulus decision table is totally logical and predictable simply because it is part of the upper level of our fantasy life. It allows us to reach back down for help into the much more powerful and unknowable Rho space.

Sometimes awareness and reality seem to be close to the same thing. Collapse by an observer is based on the wave function created at envisioning time. The imagination drives all future event collapses. Part of it is what we think we should see, so our imagination drives our next version of reality, The eyes allow us to display an image that lets us imagine the next image to be similar or

Appendix C Triverity

slightly altered by movement or external changes to the object.

Imagination also creates the bumps, the future events that we don't want in our path. We need to continually adjust the EWF from the brain, usually when we have new info that changes our perception of what the end event will or should be.

The wave functions are different from simple photon quantum collapses. They were first envisioned by the Copenhagen convention 100 years ago as a way to explain experimental quantum data results.

Once any EWF is created, the possible paths are defined by the Matrix but some paths that contain bumps may prove to be unacceptable to the brain. So how does the brain know if there are any in a given path? Either it peruses and analyzes the entire chart, or else the Matrix decides by accessing data in the brain that is quantum entangled with other brains. Actually, the brain could do a complete run through of the entire chart as soon as the Matrix gets his first pass done, a more complicated handshake operation. The EWF leading to an end event becomes smaller as time gets closer. A brain may have to move along on a path until the bump becomes too big, then try to select an alternate path. The problem we're running into here is the vast number of paths that lead to a far-off end event. It may solve that problem by returning a shorter path as best choice but the most likely path is also there. Or, the brain may analyze the entire path of these top few until it finds one that has no unacceptable bumps. Easy to do on its quantum computer.

This process gives our imagination lots of power. It creates the EWF that results in the specific events envisioned. The event should be described in as much detail as is known. If you want the basketball to go through the hoop, imagine it doing that so that the brain knows specifically what the end event looks like. If you imagine a situation, say that we win the game, the event wave function is

Appendix C Triverity

scattered over many observers and the paths to success are packed at the top. There is no obvious way for the brain to select one. Which events will have any certain effect on the end event is fuzzy. It may be undetermined or unrecognizable since winning could be taken to mean something other than what you think or wish for it to be. Indeed, there are many possible paths.

And, this is important, remember that there must be belief that it will work as envisioned.

Again, our mind does not have access to other brains' tables even though the Matrix does. So, we do not know the effect of our choices on them. We may find that to be an unacceptable bump if we knew. The Matrix knows by cross referencing other EWFs. It has to guess what will be the most likely behavior by others, so it uses the probabilities for the end event in that other one's EWF, knowing that they may not select the most probable events. It sets up our EWF as best it can, based on the very few other minds that may be involved in our event. So, maybe not such

Rhoality Guide to Wellness

a big job. In fact, if no other brain is determined that this event is important, there may not be any other EWF that addresses the same event.

It generally isn't possible that your brain is cognizant of events along the way. You have to believe that they will result in your path being followed even without specific knowledge or input. It is likely that the final correct path is unknown until much closer to the end time, especially since others have free will and may interfere. New entrants could change probabilities, so the Matrix has to continually change your actions. When that needs to happen, that's when you need to be attuned to your inner voice guardian and do as you're told.

A Rhoality life

A life of Rhoality is available to anyone with a mind open to the possibility of a creator who set things up to work in our favor. You know you live in the right mind state when you

Appendix C Triverity

spend so much time daydreaming that everyone says you live in a fantasy world. You can concentrate and focus to get back to Alpha and even Beta or snap to awareness to analyze a possible fight or flight event, but then slip back to Rho state as soon as the stimulus ends. Given time and attention, others will realize that your fantasy world is the result of your being, like the ancient Greeks, favored by the gods.

Guardianship by others

Could another person be your guardian? The power of Rhoality isn't inherent in everyone in the real world. It takes a clear, dedicated mind that believes it can do you good. Love from a good heart isn't always clear in its actions but it is almost always focused on its object and intent. If the favors you have received over a period of your life coincide with another person who seemed to be there whenever you needed someone, it's possible that they served as a Rho guardian to you. And the closer they were to being an intimate traveler, the more powerful was their influence. Chances are they also didn't realize their power. Mothers who are empaths with their children are almost certainly in the group. The EWF that collapsed in your favor may not have been envisioned by you.

We can imagine that our guardian is like the creator's personal emissary to us. It seems to keep us safe without being asked to, and perhaps we will never know what limits there are to it. We like to think that our imaginations have created so many outstanding EWF's that they hang around all our lives and play out as needed like they are being orchestrated by a personal assistant. So, we might wonder what the nature of the event wave function for Rhomers could be. What is it that creates so many of these wave functions for events that they make us feel like we have a guardian that allows us delightful daydreams, memorable night dreams, hopeful wishes and desires, fleeting joyful feelings and emotions, and entrainment with others even though mostly

Appendix C Triverity

subconscious? We build these up, adding to them all our lives and since we are balanced enough for them to take place on their own, they can happen without us having any input at all. And thus, this would be our guardian.

Guardianship for others

Rhomers are attuned to the quantum functioning of the mind and return often to the Rho state, so having a guardian is inherent and people who live in the Rho State have ready quantum access to the creation of the event wave functions. If indeed our extended time spent in the Rho State is what enables the constant management of the EWFs, then the guardian is built into Rhoality.

The guardian angel that many people sense they have may mean that they actually have Rhomers nearby that they are unaware of. It is a gift to live in one's mind. Daydreaming is heavenly and protection by a guardian follows without request.

Rhoality Guide to Wellness

A common characteristic of a guardian is an empath, one who can comprehend and feel the emotional state of someone else. Others feel a strange emotional connection to people they don't know, what we could smile and call a *Disturbance in the Force*. Once we are aware and follow up on these feelings, we learn to recognize it. Usually, we have to be near someone or in intimate contact with them. When we love someone and constantly think of them, their lives are all the better for it.

Entrainment

In physics, when two quantum particles touch, they become entangled. That means they're essentially one particle in two places, so no matter how far apart they are, anything that happens to one happens to both. That's proven quantum science. Now, when two people touch, they mingle their magnetic fields as well, which then affect each other's fields to make them more alike. That's called entrainment. So, the combination of the two causes those touching intimately to become more alike. The more they touch and the longer they're in contact, the more it happens.

Rhomers spend a lot of time in the Rho state, which is the pathway to the quantum mind. Therefore, when they come close to another Rhomer, they feel it. That's why we sometimes feel drawn to a stranger and want to touch. In fact, you might say that the best way for you to lead a happy Rhomer life is to live with your guardian.

Being a Guardian

If you are a guardian, you must have daily contact with whomever you're guarding to maximize your impact. But beware, even trying for a better future for someone else could cause harm. As a guardian we can easily still take a path and event that may not do anyone any good.

To be a guardian for someone else is an overpowering responsibility. You envision what you think will be a good return for them but being specific enough to have an effect is difficult, and even then, it may not result in the good you anticipate. In fact, you may never know if the event was successful like you wanted it, or their brain confusion rewrote the script until your event spoiled the success. If the receiver has a confused mind or your events are continually overwritten in their own state table, they will continue to create bumps in your path. Again, you have to be intimately connected to know when a bump might occur.

Emotions

Hameroff said virtually all human behavior is in some way related to the pursuit of pleasure in its various forms. On one hand, you have pleasure, on the other, anxiety and fear. How are these emotions tied in there? When you see an object, either through the eyes or from a brain creation, you attach an emotion to it. When you envision a future event happening or multiple events (situation) you attach an emotion and stash it

Appendix C Triverity

inside the EWF. Any events along the path to the final end event that you envision will have their own EWF and emotions. Normally emotions are handled by the amygdala gland but since the discovery of quantum collapses, it also has to be handled somewhere else in the mind also.

Being in the Rho state does not offset the ability of the mind to pursue the higher pleasures, that spark that makes some days simply more enjoyable than others. It motivates us to push ahead toward the kind of life we have always dreamed about, knowing that attaining our eventual life end point can be a pleasant, pain-free journey. The excitement that goes with anticipation of pleasure.

Influencing the collapse

To shrink clouds for events, many observations are required. An event collapse still has to occur when a yes/no decision is made. How do you observe any event when you can't observe situations in their entirety, only results for each intended event, then conclude success or failure yourself? You may get a good result if your events for someone close to you were to be handled by their state tables being updated by your preference as to what you would want for yourself. If they fall and land unhurt, that's the very way that you would have wanted to land. How about for somebody farther from you? If you wish for them to land safely while skydiving, you may be cognizant of the chute not being packed right or else have a vague feeling that something is wrong. At that point, the bump in the EWF path has arrived and your EWF path should know the possibilities that have not been chosen because the envisioning was started in your Rho space and maintained by your Rho Matrix.

If you look at an electron cloud of possibilities, you see an image of smudgy shells that is darker in some bands but it still extends outward, getting dimmer the farther it gets. In time, it could extend with no limit

Appendix C Triverity

until it hit the edge of the universe. Finally, at the time the event occurred, it could collapse to any of the probabilities that exist for it even out across the universe.

If some of the clouds have a lot of identical probabilities, it would make sense that the collapse could start somewhere before it is close enough for the brain or other observer to decide how it collapses.

To a photon collapse in our reality, the most interesting factor is the energy level. In any Rhoality event, the most interesting thing is success or fail at each individual event. The end of the event may never be totally what is expected.

Group Guardians

Can we use a group effort to help others? Certainly. When we envision an event for someone else, what we're really imagining is finding in our own future that our desired event has impacted another person. This sets up the EWF for them as well as us. The

Rhoality Guide to Wellness

information to create the timeline for this path is also in the Rho field, but not as clearly defined if they aren't entangled in some way with us. In fact, Rhomers are able to increase the favorability of events by sharing desires within the group, thus allowing a synergism among them all.

Others envisioning on our behalf help remove bumps in our path by altering the probabilities of events along the way, but it works both ways. Someone could put bumps in your way, so live in peace with everyone.

Rhomers almost always work for a living because they have responsibilities in their real lives. Nothing in a workday would prevent them from easing back into Rhoality whenever they choose.

Miracles

Impossible events, what we often call miracles, don't exist in Rhoality, just guidance to the best possible event outcome.

Appendix C Triverity

Rhomer Villas

To facilitate nearness and encourage closeness among people, the Rho Villa is established. It is designed to enable Rhomers and like-minded people to gather in an atmosphere of acceptance and natural beauty, all for enhancement of their understanding of what has been endowed for them by their brains. Such a place would allow the full opening of the Rhomer mind.

The existence of a Rho Villa gives life to a world where imperfect people tolerate the human frailties of each other. They spend half their Rho dream time doing for themselves and the other half doing for others. They communicate their needs and desires through envisioning them, which creates EWFs that are detectable by the others. The more entrained they are, the more they can support each other by adding the same visions.

How to create a Rho Villa

Rhoality Guide to Wellness

Functions of a Villa:

- Meeting place for like people.
- Training and discussions.
- Naturing.
- Mind channeling.
- Communion.
- Rho garden.
- Exceptionally beautiful natural settings with meditation and communion spaces.
- Games.
- Thought provoking, tuned to strengthening of mind, fun, communion.
- Climbing trees, meant for fun, exercise, naturing.
- Projects.
- Building and creating objects that improve the utility of the Villa.
- Laughter.
- Health and communion, start sessions with balanced mind.

Appendix C Triverity

- Discussions to make sense of the world and improve mind channeling.
- Good works.
- Help others outside the Rhomer group and feel good about society.
- Training for RSL (Rho State Living).
- Aid understanding of science and benefits of a balanced life.
- Books and literature.
- Everybody an authority and an author.
- Gene manipulation.
- Basics of how gene manipulation is changing our world, how to recognize gene manipulation and research into repairs.

Many Rhomers find fellow travelers to be a great help in developing and understanding living in the Rho state or simply have given in to curiosity or need to have the support of like-minded individuals, so they congregate at Rho Villas. These are often called Rho Tents from the book *Passion Spent*, a story about people who find hope and understanding at Pashan's Tent. Being in close proximity to each other reinforces the entrainment of the overlapped fields that emanate from the body's organs, particularly the brain and the heart. Activities that bring the body into contact with others in similar movements, such as close dancing, and mentally attaching to nature by touch, boost the sensitivity that is necessary to separate out emotions that lead to a positive end event. This keeps the mind eased inside the Rho state and makes rewiring of the subconscious survival programs easier.

Someone entering a Rhomer Villa can rightfully expect to find:

- Power of positive thinking.
- Synergism of group actions and abilities.
- Power of intimacy and touch.
- Encouragement toward confidence.
- Community and entrainment with nature.
- Calm, balance, coherent minds.
- Open minds to things they don't understand.
- Belief in brain healing.

Appendix C Triverity

- Belief in power greater than yourself.
- Power of love and forgiveness.
- Lack of chronic worry, anger and guilt.
- Healthy body, pain free existence.
- Discussions with others having curiosity.
- Half time for you, half for others.
- Sharing of grief and yearnings.
- Guardianship for others you care about.
- Understanding of creation of the Universe.
- Entrainment with others with like auras.
- Freedom from criticism for beliefs or seeking.
- Entrex abilities to fight brain misuse of the body.

When we step out into the sunshine, photons hit our skin and trigger our receptors. We are consciously aware of the changes, but soon it wears off and we no longer are aware of it, even though we are still conscious of it and focus on it when desired. Consciousness could be the current focus of our mind and awareness would be an input that interrupts our consciousness, or vice versa. All five (or more) senses are triggered by quantum clouds since every particle has a cloud and sensors react to particles. Some are sensor driven, even internal nerves at the bottom of it all.

Rho State Living (RSL) science - Pashan

Almost everyone here has gone through a session or taken part in the recent trials, so we can start with just a brief summary of the science behind the Rho state and its functions. Our goal is to determine the scientific basis for anything we believe. Some of it is provable with a smoking-gun type proof, which has a process that is detectable and reasonable. Others are provable by the constant results they produce but some details are undetectable or not clearly understood. We call this type of science Metascience.

I consider two possibilities here. One, the brain is able to access the information it needs to make decisions about its future,

Appendix C Triverity

thereby altering its own reality to something it likes more, or two, the cosmos software manages information contained inside the brain energy field. It determines the best path and makes them available to the brain. Both processes can be defended, and both certainly have their advantages. Yes, question?

Refer to Appendix C for Pashan's answers.

Rhoality Guide to Wellness

Table 1. Standard Rhomer Science Summary

- Creators created the universe out of a giant energy field by using basic forces to change some energy into particles and by applying electromagnetism to amass some of the new particles and to separate others. These particles emit photons in the visible light frequencies in order to be detectable by a computing machine they designed and created for just this purpose, the brain.

- The earth was created to be a living space for life, which in itself was created by the energy and particle vibration, and processes were added to living things to evolve them to higher intelligence.

- What we call matter is the brain's take on the photons of light that reach us through the body's sense organs. Most information that reaches us is either not detectable or not made available to the conscious mind.

- Physical structures in the human body support a communication path between the brain and the energy field within the brain.

Appendix C Triverity

- The brain runs and maintains the workings of the body to its maximum benefit as it understands what that is. The brain becomes unbalanced and confused when it goes into survival mode due to a perceived danger. This mode reroutes the energy of the body to the muscles and critical organs, resulting in other organs getting cut off from the normal supply of blood, toxin cleansing, and waste management.
- The body needs to come completely out of survival mode as soon as possible in order for the normal functioning to resume. Failure to do so causes inflammation, leading to dysfunction and disease.
- Because our modern world is inherently permanently stressful, the body usually does not complete the cleansing action when the brain gives a general signal to do so.
- A balanced brain, free from confusion due to anxiety and other mind demons, can heal the body and will do so as soon as it is convinced that help is on the way. Think placebo effect.
- The brain normally stays in the mid-frequency Beta state. During rest time, it falls into the

Rhoality Guide to Wellness

low frequency Delta state and when racing, it jumps up into a high-frequency Gamma state. Intermediate states allow daydreaming and meditation to access the subconscious, which allows the brain to balance, as shown by brain wave scans.

- For some people, attaining the necessary states to let the brain do its body healing isn't difficult. They have a central state, called the Rho state, to which the brain automatically reverts to when the body comes completely out of survival state. This state is sufficiently balanced to allow the brain-cosmos connection feature to fully function.

Appendix C Triverity

- **Table 2. Rhomer Metascience Summary**

- To complete the survival mode cleansing process, a conscious relaxation of the lower enteric area muscles is necessary.
- The brain connection to the cosmos is most likely a combination of the magnetic field in the brain and the entanglement of the energy in the spaces inside the atoms with the microtubules inside living cells.
- The Rho Matrix knows the paths that will be best for us.
- Energy can store a fantastic amount of information. Over the last few million years that life on Earth has existed, all the data produced by events have been stored inside this energy field. The energy inside the brain is within its magnetic field and is still entangled with the energy of the universe so its information is available for the brain to access. The Rho Matrix makes these decisions by determining all the possible paths from the current status of the brain to the goal that the brain has decided on. It keeps track of all the possible paths to the goal from

having been where the brain is now and determining how the past brains found their way to the goal. In our software, we store all the data to create the paths in the form of a state-stimulus table, which is actually a decision table, and includes the actions that have to be taken to move along the timeline laid out in each path.

- As each photon reaches the brain from matter, the brain must collapse it into its reality. An unimaginable number of photons arrive at the human eye, collected by an estimated 126 million rods and cones, which are combined into one million information sets.

- Before the brain can collapse the wavefunctions of the photons, the Matrix must set up all the possibilities inside each one. It takes the information to do this from its internal decision table, stored in the brain energy fields and possibly its DNA, and makes a list of all the possibilities, then presents it to the brain to choose from. The list is inclusive of all possibilities, provided in most probable

Appendix C Triverity

order. The brain may not select what the cosmos thinks is the best path because only the brain knows the side effects and other considerations that should go into the decision. The Matrix then updates all decision tables affected by the event collapse for the next round.

Appendix D
You the Creator

Appendix D Creator

Imagine you are the creator.

Imagine that you own a giant quantum energy field, what we might call the pre-universe. You wish to create a cosmic-type aquarium, complete with objects that move and reproduce themselves, and allow you to enjoy being an integral part of it all. How would you do it?

As Tesla said, when you think of the universe, think of energy, frequency, and vibration. You as creator have the ability to alter the nature of this energy by utilizing the (quantum) physics as it exists in your sphere. Your basic design is to create a new science that can manipulate this energy so that it can be analyzed, interpreted, and displayed to simulate a reality to the new beings in a simple setting that allows them to function, move about, and enjoy the pleasures of life such as procreation and creativity.

The challenge is great. In order to have a physical medium, what in reality is often called the cosmos, that allows your new invention to

Rhoality Guide to Wellness

be created, maintainable, and guided by you, this new science must have a set of laws that can be comprehended by the beings to the point they can survive, evolve, and increase their intelligence. To monitor these changes, you invent a sensor that can also analyze changes. what we term a brain. You connect this device to the quantum world through a consciousness.

Things that will be incomprehensible to the new brains that are a normal part of quantum physics like two objects occupying the same space or one single particle existing in more than one location, and perhaps even time itself, will have to operate smoothly in their reality but behind the scenes.

The bricks and mortar of our reality, what we call matter, will have to be made from the giant energy soup that contains so much energy that no life as you envision it could ever survive. You have to alter the nature of the energy field so that the wave function associated with the constructs you come up

Appendix D Creator

with are presented to the new beings as probabilities. The basis of the new reality will be packets of electromagnetic waves travelling from carefully crafted clumps of energy that are termed atoms.

This energy has inherent vibration and force fields that can be arranged to create the matter. You mass some together, using basic forces of nature to keep them together and help keep them apart. You begin by squeezing enough energy together to create a huge explosive alteration of energy into particles that emit photons in a very narrow frequency (energy) band that can be detected by the brain. They are so tiny that they have to coalesce by fusion into larger particles (atoms), forging an array of elements, again, by the quantum laws of physics. Nowhere along the path of this process have these laws been breached.

Creation of Life

You as creator would begin forming what we consider living objects by arranging the inherent vibrational energy of particles into objects that eventually will be able to detect changes in other objects. They do this by sensing the wave nature of the emitted photons and their associated force fields to make images that allow a connection between the objects. These images in the brain we call reality.

In order to orchestrate to a desired end, you start with a coded blueprint called DNA. You give the living cells a back door to be altered from the outside using this door to inject gene changes.

So how do you keep control of the life of living beings? The brain is in close contact with the quantum energy inside and outside of the particles in the brain, the atoms. Magnetic fields, particle entanglement, and the constant creation of new sub-atomic particles that the brain can sense, all correlate into a two-way communications path between you and your creation. Each brain has enough free will to

Appendix D Creator

help in the handshake to make its future reality a very personal process.

Free Will

So, how does free will work? Matter does not exist in the brain's reality before it it's observed by the consciousness. It comes to the brain as a cloud of probabilities, which give it a choice of realities to choose from. This is the beginning of free will on the reality side of this handshake. The other part is the consciousness that is installed in a brain, again by a handshake. By the time it is ready to be an independent entity, it may have as many consciousnesses available as deemed necessary to protect the brain from damage and to simply enable the direction its future takes.

Are there limits on this enabling process? Yes, it is not a magic wand; it cannot transgress the laws of quantum physics that were in existence at the beginning. The cloud of possibilities maintained by the creator must be possible under these laws. Note here that the gift of

Rhoality Guide to Wellness

selection of future events is the reason it was created the way it was in the first place. The gift of free will.

Is there an inherent weakness in the chosen design? Yes, all the necessary consciousnesses must be in place by the time that the survival programming is complete. It's not impossible to evolve new consciousness, but it is complex and not covered here. Rewiring subconscious programming allows the current consciousness to behave as per new programming during survival threat reactions instead of evoking a new consciousness.

To make it all accessible to a brain, you the creator change energy into atoms, which are tiny machines designed to emit different frequencies that the brain can detect. Each different elemental type of matter emits a unique frequency in order to enable the brain to make an interesting and a tunable free will reality. That collapse is based on past, present, and future data by analyzing the past, recognizing the present, and having access to

Appendix D Creator

the probable future. To allow the brain a choice in the collapse is the reason the cloud was invented.

In one sense, we can debate the chicken-and-egg question: which came first, consciousness or observer? As long as there exists a consciousness to observe, there will be something in existence to be observed by it.

Photon collapse allows for early consciousness input since the quantum fields extend beyond the brain. Therefore, the collapse of photons may begin as they near the receptors. In a sense, this makes entanglement and magnetic fields into observers. The collapse point can be anywhere within the space inside or outside the brain's area of influence, its aura.

Note that we do not capitalize the word creator because we wish to not imply that it is an object worthy of or influenced by worship. It simply doesn't care if it is or not. The system of life that it created will by design help people live the life they select for themselves and will do so if they believe and follow the process. It's all carrot and no stick.

Appendix E

Questions for Pashan

Rhoality Guide to Wellness

QUESTION: I'm thinking of doing a brain rewiring to clear out some really awful survival responses that have lost me friends over the years. It's not easy for me to hold a meditation session in a lower mental state, probably because I have trouble imagining the response I'm wanting in a consistent manner. Could a frequency rewiring help me?

ANSWER: Possibly, but the published test results only pointed to the utility of using frequency to balance the brain and less for actual DNA alteration. I would suggest you use the frequency to put yourself in the state that you can meditate as you would like and continue the repetition of accessing your decision chart whenever you feel a survival response is necessary. Look for real life situations where you can do that and if you can find a partner who really likes to push your buttons so you can practice on them or a combination might be the quickest way. By selecting the responses you want to have and

Appendix E Questions

practicing them, you redraw the decision chart that is used to determine the correct response.

QUESTION: How comprehensive does the chart need to be?

ANSWER: To begin, pick a couple of your worst responses and concentrate on them. That will begin the updating of your state-stimulus table, which is a list of the events that cause you to react and the response you want to give. As it fills out, the lesser anxiety-producing events will be that much easier to pull out as your responses become more automatic. Also, a partner would be able to rate your progress more objectively than you alone could.

QUESTION: If you want something that someone else also has asked for, how does the Rho process reconcile that?

ANSWER: If there is a conflict between Rhomers, say as a simple example, two people pushing while wanting to occupy the space the other one is in. If one outweighs the other, due to the laws of physics, the possibilities inside the photons that come to the first person don't have a very high probability, in fact, near zero, while the heavier person has maybe a higher one.

So, what we want to know is how the Rho Matrix factors that in without favoring one over the other. It is constantly testing the viability of the chosen path event possibilities to assign current numbers to them in order to rank them for both people.

When you have clarified in your mind what you want, the Matrix changes your table to reflect that, then redefines the possible and preferred paths to get there. This may result in the rewiring of the other person's data in the same way, which then alters the possibilities and preferences that it offers to them. It is automatic and doesn't mean that it plays favorites or even considers whether it is doing good or not. It flips between them until the issue is decided or abandoned. Along those lines, if timelines do exist, this would be a likely

Appendix E Questions

cause of them since each mind wants the best for its brain.

QUESTION: Does Rhoality explain why we tend to be creative?

ANSWER: Rhomers seem to groove on the opportunity to be creative. We have found two distinct types, those who can create new ways of doing things and those who can make things look good. One includes inventive people like scientists, engineers, and inventors, and the others are talented people like artists, musicians, and philosophers. Inventive people can have deep passions for a given project or problem, but as soon as the design is structured or the problem solved, the passion wanes and the mind starts looking for another challenge. This makes outsiders consider us to have a short attention span and not always in a favorable light.

Note here that a Rhomer who is mentally past the creative phase while envisioning has an increase in anxiety as they attempt to move into the construction stages. Writers often force themselves into the final preparation steps of publishing and feel great stress in the attempt.

Along these lines, Rhomers make great partnerships with others who aren't so creative but can manage the detail and repetition that drives us crazy, if each understands the other and appreciates that they may each have different perceptions of what is desirable in a symbiotic relationship.

QUESTION: Is there physical proof for the brain-cosmos connection?

ANSWER: I can see two possibilities for accepting the proof by looking at outcomes. One is the design and structure of the brain and other parts of the body that create methods of connection, such as the brain's synthesis of magnetite. It creates a magnetic field that is detectable from outside the body and the only reasonable use for it is to overlap and probably interface with other fields, inside and outside the body. The other proof is

Appendix E Questions

anecdotal, meaning that people have experienced things in their lives that point to and can only be explained by the brain's ability to use information stored somewhere, most likely in the space in the atoms of the brain: the Rho space.

As long as it works for someone, we have to keep our minds open as to its nature and whether it could work for anyone else. Remember, all human brains have a lot of common functions, but people are still unique individuals with unique survival programming and experiences, and as we age, our bodies change in unknown ways, so their use of mental facilities is also bound to change. So don't expect to be able to repeat someone else's successes, just keep going until you find your own.

QUESTION: How could the future reality possibly be changed without transgressing the laws of physics?

ANSWER: Information stored in the brain's Rho space (as used here, energy space inside and

Rhoality Guide to Wellness

around the atoms of the brain) goes back millions of years and contains all the previous events from that time. Given all the various ways that the brain could access data stored inside energy, it should be possible for a quantum computer like the one in the Rho Matrix to analyze that data, looking for similar situations, stimuli (arriving cloud of possibilities), and reality.

These computers, possibly contained in the microtubules inside the brain, calculate all the possible paths (event sequences) of all these events. Any of them that lead to the goal presented by the mind is given a high probability and put in the decision table (here a simple state table) along with the reality state of the brain and any stimuli that would move reality toward the next event in the path. The mind then uses the table to select the most probable event that leads down the path with the least side effects, then collapses the stimulus to create that reality.

Appendix E Questions

If the brain is coherent and in resonance with its environment, achieved by the conscious mind providing an explicit and well-defined goal, it will update the table accurately for the next stimulus. If not, random entries are made which keep the brain confused. Remember, reality is just the brain's take on the stimuli it receives. It is free to create any reality it chooses, so long as it obeys the laws of physics.

As an aside, if there are creators who maintain the earth for life to continue, it's a small step to think they meddle and even manipulate our reality. It's then an even smaller step to belief that they allow us to do so.

This was a fairly straightforward explanation of how our mind can take advantage of the brain's ability to access information stored in energy fields within and possibly outside itself, to help us determine our future. The other side of the question is how our mind can influence decisions made by other brains when there is no connection besides quantum entanglement. Indeed, it would have to alter multiple decision tables, unknown to ourselves. This would only

Rhoality Guide to Wellness

be possible if the Rho Matrix updated everyone's tables for all events and allowed our decisions to affect all of them.

QUESTION: Are there new physical laws created for this?

ANSWER: No, the cosmos has to obey its own laws that it set out at the beginning, even in the quantum world. Therefore, for it to be able to input information into the mind, it has to have a pre-set process that it follows, most likely something like the state tables we use. They explain where this data is stored, where it came from, and physically how the brain could access it. It also shows why the brain does things that are best explained by the connection, such as why it synthesizes magnetite and why the pineal gland has piezoelectric crystals, both of which are designed to create a magnetic field. The brain will follow these laws, as it knows best the physical state of the body and what the mind wants.

Appendix E Questions

QUESTION: Why did the creator design collapsible clouds of possibilities instead of solid objects?

ANSWER: The fact that our reality is based on the collapse of the clouds of possibilities by the mind shows how the design of the whole process would lead to decisions about events in the future, which lies in what the mind considers best for itself and its body. This is called free will.

These freely taken choices result in a process that gives brains and bodies health and longer pain-free lives. The mystery here is why aren't brains given an innate knowledge of these features, so they could be better used by everyone. As we quoted before, everything collapsed by the brain seems to be somehow related toward the pursuit of pleasure in one of its many forms. Unfortunately, some forms of pleasure are at cross purposes with our life goals. Even if reality is an illusion in our own version of it, we still have to consider the reality of other people in order to balance our

Rhoality Guide to Wellness

brains to maximize the future for ourselves. Harming someone else is the surest way to brain decoherence.

QUESTION: Can two auras entrain?

ANSWER: Surely. The brain's aura includes a magnetic field that can be detected several feet outside the body. Other auras certainly overlap with it and these fields affect each other. People who spend a lot of time in intimate contact with others tend to take on similar characteristics. I can't imagine a limit to it. It depends a lot on the amount of time together and the desire and belief of the individuals involved. Feelings like sadness when you don't know why are often the result of two auras entrained without knowing it.

QUESTION: what is mind channeling?

ANSWER: Focusing on another's mind to gain entrainment. Rhomers often report feeling an emotion-like connection when they come in close contact with like minds. In the media, it

Appendix E Questions

has been described as a disturbance in the force. Perhaps a little flighty, but when you think about it, that is a good description.

QUESTION: What is consciousness?

ANSWER: Quantum physics tells us that the truth about our physical existence is that our universe is made up of countless bits of energy, all clumped together into what we call atoms and emitting light that our brain can detect. Circe defined consciousness as the connection between truth and reality, with truth being the energy at the bottom of it all and reality being the images painted inside our brains. Truth makes reality possible. They are not the same thing. Consciousness is the missing factor between the two that makes it work. It is more than simply awareness. The brain is aware of many things that never make it into our conscious mind.

The physical brain is created according to the laws of physics, then somewhere in the process of a single cell turning into a human body, a consciousness is added. The notion of

Rhoality Guide to Wellness

self is a physical survival definition, more than staying alive. To create events, energy has to be moved around, but only within the laws of physics. These laws are never abridged or overwritten, not even by the creators.

QUESTION: How does the Retron process work?

ANSWER: The Retron process is standard during normal cell mitosis and how we use it is the same as standard CRISPR except that we don't have to cut the DNA, we simply wait until the cell goes through normal mitosis division and slip the patch into it. It makes for more straightforward patch acceptance but the effects take more time to express.

QUESTION: Does having a quantum mind state that we can access mean that other disciplines that use reality mind state functions are invalid?

ANSWER: Not at all. They more often than not use the focusing of energy in the brain to aid and even heal problems in the body. However,

Appendix E Questions

the problems that are actually caused by the brain can only be healed by removing the need for this energy everywhere except for the brain. It remains there, allowing a balanced and coherent mind to refrain from creating them.

QUESTION: What is a biobank?

ANSWER: A biobank is a genetic storage location for stem cells, particularly for humans. Stem cells taken in youth are frozen and are available for medical use in later life. This is particularly useful when gene tampering is suspected. Pashan's Tents all have access to this service through our private genetic laboratory.

QUESTION: Homo sapiens is the only surviving branch of humanity out of many. Is it the last?

ANSWER: Surely not. Someone has put too much effort into getting us this far to abandon us now. But we have essentially halted any of their intrinsic evolution, so no more survival of

Rhoality Guide to Wellness

the fittest. The next branch will be gene-engineered by advanced humans for their own purposes. When one of the global power groups prevails, the others will all be gene-edited into no further possibility of evolving. Now to speculate, the humans to be selected to continue evolution must have a connection to the creator. The best-postured ones for this would undoubtedly be the Rhomers.

QUESTION: Is an event collapse handled by the subconscious?

ANSWER: Event collapses are many and continuous, but very little of what occurs actually reaches the conscious mind. The reason we don't have feelings or knowledge of having made more decisions is that the collapse decision is handled by the Rho Matrix, which is quantum and analogous to the subconscious mental state. Actually, that's what Power the Quantum Mind says.

QUESTION: Does the event collapse show up on the brain wave chart?

Appendix E Questions

ANSWER: Any quantum occurrence happens much too quickly to be detected by machine. Photons are emitted by atoms at something like 10 followed by 20 zeros per second.

QUESTION: How can science operate with two different sets of laws, quantum and classic, one at a human level and another that subatomic particles obey?

ANSWER: In all, it is no mystery why physics is divided into two incompatible sets of laws; one is a simple subset of the other. But there is a connection: quantum physics allows, indeed requires, that an observer, surely a consciousness housed in a mind, observe the output of a quantum action in order for it to become a part of the higher system that we call reality. This would seem to make everything at human reality level an illusion without substance. For that observer, however, life is full of countless other brains, each with its own consciousness. Reality must have been provided with a framework to allow constancy to life that would allow the brain to find balance and cohesion with the material world and with other brains. So from the vantage point of the creators, that predictability, cause and effect would keep us all on the same page and allow the cognizant brain to take advantage of the process that the creator has provided. This would allow us to help determine our own futures.

QUESTION: Why can't our brains understand quantum science?

ANSWER: The creators gave the brain a physical body in order to connect with and control the physical world around them. At no time did they envision that their apex creation, humans hopefully, would ever need to comprehend anything below or beyond that. Suddenly, after millions of years of evolution, the brain developed to the point it could discover the quantum world, then wanted knowledge of how it works. This would seem to indicate that for humans to progress into a

Appendix E Questions

full understanding of how the universe works, a new and better brain will be needed.

We have a theory on how that will be accomplished. Past world history would seem to show that the amount of oxygen in the air is what allows higher life to materialize from lower species. Twice the planet was frozen over and returned to normal but with higher levels of oxygen, first around 3%, then it moved that up to 20%. So, it stands to reason that a higher-level brain would require the earth to have a higher level of oxygen. Apparently, it would require something as drastic as a snowball Earth to achieve that. If our consciousness comes from the creators, then this insane drive for humans to build tools that will lead to our own destruction could be on them, not us. On purpose! It would be a nuclear winter caused by our bombs, the next snowball Earth.

QUESTION: Does the brain make pre-packaged decisions?

Rhoality Guide to Wellness

ANSWER: To answer that, we need to look at the wave nature of reality. It isn't a solid object. It indicates that a lot of every decision made by a brain originates from information received as a cloud of possibilities that the mind is free to choose from. This allows each brain to guide its future events by analyzing the cloud and after considering the moral and preferential consequences of each possibility, selecting the one that gets it to its stated aim and predetermined goal. The end event or state of satisfaction is set up by the brain in its balanced and believing state.

QUESTION: How does the Rho Matrix handle morality?

ANSWER: The quantum world has no morality, which is simply the emotion our mind connects to each reality image at its creation time. At that moment when we envision an event, the wave function is formed by the brain and is processed by the Rho Matrix, what we have defined as the software being run by the brain

Appendix E Questions

and accessing the information stored in the energy inside the brain in Rho space. The ranking of possibilities in each event cloud is made on what the brain defines as what it wants and what the Rho Matrix thinks is the most efficient way of arriving there.

QUESTION: Is this process similar to software running on a computer?

ANSWER: Not a simple question, so let's go into this in a lot of detail here. Classical physics sitting atop a quantum physics base could be described in detail by depicting it as being analogous to a software app running on a processor.

The app creates processes that perform the desired algorithmic functions. How they do that is of no interest to the calling app. All it cares about is the result of the action and is not concerned about how the Rho Matrix determines the makeup of the cloud. When given options about the next event collapse, it then selects the best choices and presents them back to the Matrix for it to record the result of the collapse. The conscious mind updates reality and the Matrix updates the truth.

To determine the paths to the goal, the brain checks all the possibilities and ranks the endpoints by probability of success and critical steps in the path to the end event.

The brain has its own determination mechanism when an envision is imagined. When it envisions an event or collection of collapse results (called a situation) in the future, it lays it out for its own clarity and for the Matrix. To determine the possible paths, the Matrix searches its own database to find a similar result and then plugs in the possible paths to that event. This could be done by the entanglement and the magnetic field inside the brain, and the entanglement between the brain neurons and the Rho field (energy field in the brain space). This intimate contact between the two worlds, when you envision, causes it to imprint on the DNA.

Appendix E Questions

Lanza describes it as building a cognitive model of reality inside the brain. It gets updated during the years of intimacy with structures of the universe. So, just as a classic computer program sends constant values down to the brain and receives back the variable unknowns at envisioning time, the brain receives data from the Rho Matrix which matches end event goal to known paths to create a possibility cloud that has a wave function. This path remains in the table until new data is sent by the consciousness. It must be the same mechanism as quantum collapse. Note here that these are simply possible results, each with a probability of success, which is never 100%.

Software programmers would be quick to recognize that this is a process that calls for a state stimulus table. When the brain receives a stimulus, it digs into its memory to retrieve its predetermined response. This is because it may not have time to gather facts before it needs to make a collapse decision. To our eyes, the stimulus would be one of many photons

Rhoality Guide to Wellness

coming as a cloud of probability waves from countless atoms within our visual range. It also depends on the current state of the brain and body. A set of actions is quickly arrived at and executed, then the brain goes into a wait state for the next stimulus. The next one could be any of many possibilities, and each one must be addressed in the decision table. If the stimulus is a cloud of probability waves, the brain must select one of the possibilities and use the data contained therein to create an image for the mind and also store it as a memory. This selection results in what is termed a quantum event collapse. The stimulus cloud and the state change in our reality. The changes are made available to the Rho Matrix for it to alter its own perception of events so it can prepare for the next stimulus it needs to deal with. All straightforward so far. The sticky part is to determine who or what decides which possibilities are to be included in the cloud. For this information to be of maximum usefulness to our brain, it must contain all possibilities for the next event,

Appendix E Questions

ranked in some order of probability or utility. Thus, something outside our consciousness must know and track events in order to keep current. This intelligence is the quantum computing function in the Rho Matrix, which resides in the Rho field in the brain.

QUESTION: Why aren't all requests for future events fulfilled?

ANSWER: Unbalanced, decohered, conflicted, disbelieving brains confuse the mind.

QUESTION: Why do placebos not work sometimes:

ANSWER: Like the failed visions, doubt and disbelief kill the effect.

QUESTION: How do you alter DNA to make people into docile robots?

ANSWER: The ancient Egyptians were apparently able to do so by puncturing the amygdala gland. Same target for gene tampering?

Rhoality Guide to Wellness

QUESTION: What is the book *Power of the Quantum Mind* about?

ANSWER: The universe in all its unfathomable mystery is the cosmos. The ancient Greeks liked lucky people because they believed they were favored by the gods. Well, we all know people who are obviously favored by what we might perceive as the gods, which to these people is in fact the cosmos itself. We give our brain credit for being an unimaginably powerful machine, which it is, but it has access to and perhaps even controls an even more powerful entity, the unseen universe around us. This book explores this connection and details both the scientific basis for that power and how these lucky people came to be favored by it. We will describe how it is still accessible to us today through the mind and then introduce a new paradigm that explains how and why so many people still have the favor of the gods to this day.

Appendix F

Appendix F
Definitions

Rhoality Guide to Wellness

Dictionary of Rhoality Terms

Aura – magnetic field emanating from the body, created by magnetite synthesized by organs. P 8

Auto-immune disease – condition where your immune system mistakenly damages healthy cells.

Balance – freedom from the effect of disturbing stimuli.

Belief – the absence of doubt.

Beyond perception – a stimulus that is below or above the given range for the Rho Matrix to make the conscious mind immediately aware of it.

Biofield – aura around body.

Brain miscue – mistaken action by the brain to a stimulus, caused by decoherence and confusion.

Bump – In a Rho Vision path, an event that would negate the success of the end event.

Appendix F

Classical physics – science of matter, built atop of and supported by quantum physics.

Coherence – the trait of a wave where all peaks and valleys line up vertically.

CRISPR – Clustered Regularly Interspaced Short Palindromic Repeats. Basically, a repeating string of DNA used by the cell in DNA updates. Used by bacteria to maintain maps of virus DNA to allow it immunity from viral entry. Also used to denote a gene-editing function using this method.

Daydream – most common form of envisioning.

End event – the final event in a Rho Vision.

End event collapse – the selection by the brain of the situation at the end event, sent to the Rho Matrix.

Entanglement – for our purposes, it means that two particles that are quantum entangled each detect any event that happens to either one is the same as if it had happened to them both. At the base level, it says that a large enough quantum

Rhoality Guide to Wellness

computer can access all of the particles in the universe simultaneously.

Entrainment - merging of two auras as a result of overlapping auras.

Entrex – process of using the enteric relaxation process to bring the body out of survival state.

Entrex signals – brain-induced miscues that are signs that the body needs an Entrex.

Envisioning – process of mentally creating an intention to a desired event in the future.

ERP – Event-Related Potential – electrical activity in the brain as measured by an EEG.

Error Related Negativity (ERN) – brain pulse that occurs after initial decision on response to stimulus. In Rhoality, is the final selection of the event collapse after emotion is considered.

Event – happening after the application of an emotion to an occurrence in Rhoality.

Event path – events leading to an end event.

Appendix F

EWF – Event wave function - similar to particle wave function, physics description of the wave function associated with a future event.

Facility strength – maximum you can expect from your body's mental and physical capabilities.

Flow – in Rhoality, life's path over time. Based on emotional judgement of events being positive or negative.

Free Will – application of emotion to a possible future event.

Frequency – wave feature, described by cycles per second. Flip side of wavelength. The smaller the wavelength, the higher the frequency.

Gold fever – mental state when brain overloads on the possibility of great personal gain.

Guardianship – using Rhoality to improve events for someone else.

Healer – person with developed coherence in personal aura. Can entrain by nearness.

Rhoality Guide to Wellness

Instinct – ability to understand based on past, present and future knowledge.

Intuition – ability to understand without conscious reasoning or evidence.

Life flow potential – sum total of your physical and mental capability at any point in time. The best you can be. Exceeding this creates risk and is counter-productive because you will return to your life flow line anyway.

Luck – when preparation meets opportunity. You make the preparation and Rhoality provides the opportunity.

Majesty – feeling that you are the right one to make a decision. In Rhoality, tied in with a quiet faith in the future.

Murphy's Second Law – the more you fear something, the likelier it is to happen.

Observer – consciousness that oversees the outcome of a decision. Nothing exists in the universe until it is observed.

Appendix F

Observer collapse - in quantum physics, when the observer causes the selection of one possibility, it is turned into reality.

Occurrence – in Rhoality, change in a reality situation. Each video image frame that our eyes disclose to us can be an occurrence.

Particle - small unit of mass resulting from an observation of a unit of energy which results in its wave nature being altered to a particle nature.

Placebo effect – where a patient is cured after receiving a false treatment but believing it was real.

Plays out – In Rhoality, the process used by the Rho Matrix to determine the end event of a Rho Vision.

Quantum Cloud – list of possible states of a wave. Its collapse changes the wave nature to a particle nature.

Quantum collapse - matter begins existence as a cloud of possibilities. Observing it causes it to collapse to one of the possible states. The term

Rhoality Guide to Wellness

quantum collapse means selection of one of many possibilities.

Reality – the human perception of the result of classical science. Perceived mainly by the five senses, it results in a video being flashed into the eyes of how the brain wants to present the stimuli from the quantum objects we call matter.

Resonance – an object resonates when it receives energy that matches its own resonant frequency, absorbing it.

Rho flow line - life flow line based on our perception of negative and positive events in our lives.

Rho Space – space in the brain containing energy that is packed with historical information amassed during past eons.

Rho Matrix – software running in quantum part of the brain. Has access to body stimuli, both externally through the five senses and internally through the brain reality functions and

Appendix F

connections to age-old information stored in the brain space (Rho Space).

Rho State – a quantum mental state analogous to the reality Theta state but dealing with the quantum processes.

Rhoality - the quantum functioning of the brain. Based around the Rho mental state and input from the software called the Rho Matrix, it is the connection between classical and quantum science and is basic to the creation of matter from energy in reality.

State machine – formally, the software that runs a state-stimulus table that handles previously determined actions to stimuli.

Subliminal – stimuli below the frequency of the five senses.

Superposition – for Rhoality purposes the ability of particles to be in more than one place at a time in the quantum world.

Survival mode – state the body's subconscious mind goes into when it determines a threat to itself.

Rhoality Guide to Wellness

Yin/yang cycles – in eastern methodology, positive and negative cycles of life.

Vibes – amorphous feeling beyond conscious awareness. Often the result of instinct or intuition.

Wave nature – a wave is a disturbance that propagates. Pictured in reality as a repeating up/down line. All particles also have a wave nature and thus a wave function.

Wave function - physics term containing the description of a wave. Equal to its probability of having the sought-after characteristic.

Wellness – process of acquiring and maintaining health.

Appendix F